ecomuseum :

PERSPECTIVES IN INDIA

ecomuseum :

PERSPECTIVES IN INDIA

SANGEETA DUTTA

AGAM KALA PRAKASHAN
DELHI-110052

First Published : 2010

ISBN :978- 81-7320-102-8

Published by :
Dr. Agam Prasad, M.A., Ph.D., Diploma in Museology
for **Agam Kala Prakashan**
34, Central Market, Ashok Vihar, Delhi-110052
Ph. : 27212195, 47098550, 65688806-7
Fax : 91-11-27212195
E-mail : agambooks@gmail.com, agambook@yahoo.com
Website : www.agamkala.com

Laser Typesetting by :
Elegant Printographics
319, IIIrd Floor, R.G. Complex-I,
Sector-14, Rohini, Delhi-85.
Ph. : 9891247305

Printed at :
Chawla Offset Printers
Delhi - 110052

Printed in India

Dedicated
to
Lord Doul Govinda

Contents

Preface

Museums of 21st century are no more 'object centre' institutions, instead, they have acknowledged the idea of public service and have become 'community centered' institutions. This new development in the field of museums is known as 'new museological' development which gained popularity between 1970's-1980's.

The present study deals with ecomuseum, the concept evolved from the theory of New Museum. The new trends in museum development and the role of the community to preserve and promote its cultural and natural heritage led to the establishment of ecomuseum. An ecomuseum recognizes the importance of culture in the development of self identity and its role in helping a community to adjust to rapid changes while preserving their own culture or tradition. The ecomuseum thus becomes a tool for the economic, social, cultural and political growth and development of the society within a given social and environmental settings. Ecomuseum is often confused with New Museology. New Museology is the theory and it is a much wider phenomenon, while Ecomuseum is a part of this bigger umbrella.

New Museology is all about engaging communities and hence there seems a strong bond to ecomuseum. Certainly both emerged from the widespread dismay within the museum profession regarding the inability of museums to deal with the contemporary social, cultural, environmental, political and economic changes that confronted them in the post war years. By 1972 Santiago meeting, the word ecomuseum had been coined as a more glamorous term for the integrated museum. The term 'Ecomuseum' was accidentally given by Huges de Varine in 1971 but the concept was developed by Georges Henri Riviere much earlier.

Ecomuseum might be interpreted as a territory or territorial heritage museum. Ecomuseum has to be extended to a larger area covering it with scattered or distributed units or facilities. All such facilities though away from one another, must offer services to the public according to their needs and requirements. So the Ecomuseum is not monolithic in structure, it functions as a territory museum.

Today the image of a place is also defined by aspects which go beyond the geographic landscape and environment as such and embody other material and immaterial heritage features such as architecture, life and working practices, local products, language and oenological traditions. The Ecomuseum, as an institution which is by its very nature evolutionary and bound to the transformations of society, has thus become a key to interpreting place, hence a tool and project to give significance to the heritage features which combine to define the identity of places.

Ecomuseum have come up in different parts of the world on different lines to suit local requirements. Hence, there is no single model which can be prescribed universally to meet the requirements of all the people and lands. There is no uniformity in types, scopes and even functions in various ecomuseums. The first museums to be defined as 'Ecomuseum' were set up at Le Creusot in 1974 and in the Grande Lande in 1975.

This concept has been experimented in Indian context as there is no ecomuseum in true sense in India in spite of having broader connotations. The concept can be experimented in India in multiple ways. I have explored the facets and an attempt has been made to test the concept on the Doul Govinda sacred complex of North Guwahati, Assam against the parameters of ecomuseums postulated by western Museologists. Doul Govinda as a sacred complex an exclusive area covering north Guwahati on the north bank of the river Brahmaputra is a significant territory both culturally and ecologically which reveals a distinct local identity. The territory is noted for its vaishnava characteristics resulting in tangible and intangible heritages, historical, archaeological, cultural, linguistic as well as typical north east river ecology. There lie all the ingredients of an ecomuseum in this designated territory. The intimate association of local communities in preserving their heritage both ecological and cultural and also providing local people with an opportunity to disseminate the significant aspects of habitat and the life style in the Doul Govinda social, cultural and religious contour superimposition of the eco museum concept is addressed here along with the review of previous works on ecomuseum carried out in India and the methodology covered in the present study.

The present work is the result of the research work I carried out for the fulfillment of Doctorate Degree in Museology from National Museum Institute, New Delhi. The work was completed in 2007 but could not be published so long for numerous reasons. It has now been possible with the encouragement of the Agam Kala Prakashan. However, a few portion of the thesis has only been incorporated here. As the data collected long back, many updates have been made. In preparing this work all available source materials of primary and secondary importance have been carefully examined before use. But in spite of my sincere efforts, error may have crept into the volume for which I owe an apology to the learned readers. Again, there are increasing numbers of edited volumes available in libraries or in the market covering different aspects of ecomuseum, heritage and other relevant issues. I am sincerely not intended to compete with them. In fact it would be worth to consider as an introductory or grass root level of work with an expectation to build a foundation for new generation of museum professionals. The foundation, which will act as encouragement to start their intellectual journey. Learned readers are welcome to supplement their suggestions.

I start my work with a heartfelt thanks to all who encouraged me throughout.

Budh Purnima
The 27th of May 2010

Sangeeta Dutta
Delhi

Acknowledgements

With a deep sense of gratitude and indebtness I would like to offer my sincere thanks to Prof. A.K. Das, who remained my Supervisor, without whose valuable guidance and immense cooperation this work would not have been a complete one.

I am indebted to Mrs. Anamika Pathak, the true inspiration and energy and push factor behind this work. It is her encouragement and blessings that led me to think for this publication.

My offer of gratitude goes to the academic and administrative staff of National Museum Institute, New Delhi and the library staff of National Museum Institute and National Museum. I am thankful to my students who always demanded a comprehensive book on ecomuseum, which motivated me to prepare this work. My special thanks to Rosy, Subha and Rige for their inputs; Subhra Devi for the splendid photographs and Abhijeet for the beautiful cover design. I am also thankful to Mrs. Lila Devi and Pankaj for their support.

This work would not have been possible without the cooperation, support and care of the people of North Guwahati, Assam. Their valuable information have become the source of my knowledge. My key informers specially, Shri Paresh Bora, Shri Diganta Bardoloi, the priests and other members of the Doul Govinda temple committee, the bearers of Block

Development Office will always remain the source of my strength of research.

Let me take the opportunity to thank my family and friends who stood by me throughout. Regards to my parents and my husband Jatin. This piece of work is the result of their inspiration and blessings. Thanks and love to my little daughter Anweshaa for sparing me time to concentrate on my work.

Finally, I appreciate and offer my sincere regards to Dr. Agam Prasad of Agam Kala Prakashan for his cooperation and support, without which I would not have been able to provide it to learned readers.

(Sangeeta Dutta)
Delhi

List of Illustrations

Chapter 1

Introduction

Genesis of Museum

Museums hold their possessions in trust for humankind and for the future welfare of the human race. Their value is in direct proportion to the service they render to the emotional and intellectual life of the people.

The word museum had a variety of meanings through the ages. In classical times it signified as a temple dedicated to the Muses; nine Goddesses who preside over the epic, music, love poetry, oratory, history, tragedy, comedy, dance and astronomy. History says Alexandria, Egypt as the first organized museum like institutions established in about 3rd Century BC by Ptolemy. It was destroyed during civil disturbances 600 years later. The museum had some objects, but it was primarily a university or center for knowledge. It was an institute of philosophical study supported by the state with many prominent scholars in residence.

Euclid headed the Mathematics Department and Archimedes was on the faculty.

Following this early museum that focused on knowledge, there was a long period of museological abeyance. Although objects of various kinds were gathered in many parts of the world, most of these were either hoard collections accumulated for the monetary value of the objects or collections of curiosities gathered for their uniqueness. In neither case it was the primary motive of human enlightenment.

Evolution of Museum in Time and Space

In Europe Renaissance marked as the new changes in museum movement along with the advancement of fine arts and science, there occurred changes in the process of collection. It was a time of great change that revised the world thinking and to stress the importance of the role of human knowledge and individual experience in the process of knowing. The focus shifted from a social milieu to universal experience of human being. In the 15th cent. Florence was the center of intellectual growth that supported the best of the arts and sciences and the word 'museum' was first used here to describe the collection of the Medici during the time of Lorenzo the Magnificent. Thus the concept of museum as institutions of enlightenment had emerged.

In between the Medici Gallery of 15th cent. and the 'public' museum of 17th century there were a number of intermediate steps. In mid 20th cent. a number of external factors like funds, media, technology etc. affected the museum community. Museums then reacted to their constituency and at the same time came to realize that they had a viable product to share with their visitors – i.e. education. Museums realized that they must be very clear about their purposes. Things must be understood before they can be interpreted. The recognition of cultural pluralism has served as the basis for collections, exhibitions and new museums. Museums as centers for learning and information were established to tell the story of man and nature. Along with the changes brought in by the world in every human endevours, museums also expanded their role according to the need of the society. This situation had involved museum to rethink and redefine parameters that were thought to be permanent. Some called this development as a new paradigm within the discipline of museology. This resulted in a shift from 'object centered' museum to 'community centered' institutions. Thus, museums started involving representatives of the community and cultural group in the research and documentation.

Transformation from collection to community

The cultural experience of the community helps in a big way the understanding of museums holdings. The concept of 'public service' has become the focal point for museums and museum professionals. The changing attitudes and practices of museums reflected in the concept - the audience is supreme. Museums of early phases, which were open for a particular class of the society, now more involved in serving common mass. Basic role of museums has changed into an educational institute. It is not a conventional educational institute, but it provides education along with pleasure and enjoyment.

Development of the new museum theory

While considering the idea of public service, museums have come to acknowledge the fact that museums are people centric. In course of time we notice more and more people centric museums such as ecomuseum, community museum, neighbourhood museum, open-air museum so on and so forth. These new developments gained popularity between 1970's-1980's, to be later called 'New Museology'.

Thus, the role of museums have undergone many changes right from the museum of Alexandria to the museums of 21st century. However the close ties that exist between the development of a society and the institutions of culture that represent that society are now well known. Progress has been made towards full utilization of museums as institution of learning and social developments. However, most museums have a long way to go to meet their full potential as focused in the definition by ICOM 'museum is a non profit making, permanent institution in the service of the society and of its development, open to public, which acquires, conserves, researches, communicates and exhibits the tangible and intangible heritage of humanity and its environment for the purposes of education, study and enjoyment.

The present study involves the experimentation of ecomuseum in Indian context, the concept that developed during 1970's and which had little impact on India. The concept is associated with the role of museums in the service of the community. An ecomuseum recognizes the importance of culture in the development of self identity and its role in helping a community to adjust to rapid change while preserving their own culture or tradition. The ecomuseum thus becomes a tool for the economic, social, cultural and political growth and development of the society within a given social and environmental settings.

The concept of ecomuseum is relatively a new dimension in the field of museums in India. Though prominent museologists of India who are putting their maximum effort to familiarize this concept in Indian context, with little success. In this context attempt has been made to discuss the concept of ecomuseum worldwide and in Indian context. In Indian context the ecomuseum has a broader connotation. Here every cultural and environmental settings are already spontaneously serving as an ecomuseum within a traditional tribal village, a sacred complex, a historically significant neighbourhood, sanctuaries, mountain abode, river island, traditional industrial sites etc. The concept can be experimented in India in multiple ways. In the present study it has been explored in a sacred complex of North Guwahati, Assam.

Chapter 2

New Museum

Definition and Development

The museum philosophy and practice of late 20th century witnessed the link with post modernism, or in other words, with 'new museum'. The term 'new museum' had been used in museological literature in different ways. Some were in the view that new museum is the development of new theories and techniques to enable museums to communicate more effectively with the visitors. Again it is said new museum specifically questions traditional museum approaches to issues of value, meaning, control, interpretation, authority and authenticity. Many scholars consider the rise of the ecomuseum as tangible evidence of new museum and the history of the two concepts is closely linked. Certainly both emerged from the widespread dismay within the museum profession regarding the inability of museums to deal with the contemporary socio-cultural, environmental, political and economic changes that confronted them in the post war years. Hugues de Varine (1996:21-26) has suggested that new museology was the result of a long process during the 1960's that laid the foundation for a new approach to museums, with a strong link to the politics of development. De Varine is anxious to make a clear distinction between new museology as a movement and ecomuseum. He said the term ecomuseum should not be mixed up, which is a convenient and fashionable word, with the basic principles of new museology. They are not the same concept. Ecomuseums must be perceived as just one way in which museum professionals responded to the needs of society.

Socio- economic and political factors are responsible for the new Museology movement. Great dissatisfaction among the museologists about the passive role of the traditional museums and they also failed to create the link between the museum and community. A need was felt to cater to the need of preservation of all cultures and sub-cultures of the minorities, tribal people, etc. as the neglect or destruction of the cultural wealth of any group is a loss to the culture of the world. The need was felt that all culture be recognized, respected and appreciated as the right of each group of people. All cultures form part of the common heritage of mankind, thus the need was felt that museums must strive to help different people to trace their culture identity. Museums need to become the active agent of the overall development of society. Need for fresh paradigms and new models which could preserve the human heritage along with socio-economic development.

New Museology actually follows the tradition among museum people dating back to the 19th cent. of considering the museum as an educational institution in the service of society.

The term "New Museology' has been introduced in museological literature at least three different times at three different places, the use of the term is connected with the changing role of museums in education and in the society at large. Current museum practices are considered obsolete and the whole attitude of the professional is criticized. The profession is urged to renew itself in the perspective of a new social commitment.

- The term New Museology was first introduced in the United States at the end of the 1950s when the concept of the museum as educational institution was brought into light again.
- The second time was at the end of 1970s when in France the social role of museums was re-defined by a new generation of progressive museologists.
- Finally at the end of the 1980s the term appeared in UK in connection with a re-assessment of the educational and social role of museums in the post war period.

The Nouvelle Museology was officially founded in Marseilles in 1982; in Great Britain the term New Museology was introduced in 1989 from the book of the same title by Peter Vergo. The new Museum does not see itself as an alternative to the established museum but as a supplement opening up new dimensions.

The discourse of new Museology is essentially cultural political, not scientific. De Varine admits the difficulty of defining the essential features of New Museology "there are no established rules or models, just theories that have been immediately belied by practice"...

In New Museology the museological objectives are geared towards community development, hence the term 'Community Museology'.

- Presentation and preservation of the heritage are considered within the context of social action and change
- Heritage is a resource to be considered and developed within the context of social action and change
- The community itself has to take care of their own heritage hence the term 'Popular Museology'.
- The concept of museum is not confined to a building. The museum can be anywhere and everywhere within a specified territory. It is the French concept of 'musologie nouvelle' that gradually became recognized as one of the main streams within Museology.
- The essential feature of new Museology, as originally conceived was that museums should serve the present and future needs of their communities. Thus ecomuseum was created at a time when

environmentalism was achieving great prominence. Hugues De Varine and Georges Henri Riviere were central of the development of new ideas about museums, including the ecomuseum.

While preserving the material achievements of past civilization and protecting the achievements of the aspirations and technology of today, the new museology, eco museology, community museology and all other forms of active museology is primarily concerned with community development, reflecting the driving forces in social progress and associating them in its plans for the future. New museology demands museum's relation with their communities and also a social and economic role. The growing dissatisfaction of museologist and the people with the passive role of the traditional museum was one of the foremost reasons which led to the growth of new Museology.

Originally, new museology was about engaging communities and hence there seems a strong bond to ecomuseums and other forms of community museums and also to the integrated museum (first described in Santiago). However, in the new millennium, new museology appears much more than a just community museology and any radical changes from 'standard' philosophy and practice now appears to be enveloped within it. The new Museology originally conceived was the museums should serve the present and future needs of their communities.

The essential features of the new museology as originally conceived was the museums should serve the present and future needs of their communities. By 1972 Santiago meeting, the word ecomuseum had been coined as a more glamorous term for the integrated museum.

Rene Rivald, a prominent museologist from Canada observes that the modifier 'new' to Museology tells us practically nothing except that there must be an 'old' Museology somewhere, further compounding the problem. Most of the museologists all around the globe, thus take the word 'New Museology' not as a new science but a new movement within the realm of Museology. But it does have fundamental differences, both in theory and practice to the existing science of Museology.

A New Museology movement was first brought to public and international attention in 1972 at the round- table of Santiago (Chile) organized by ICOM. The conference emphasized on the interdisciplinary approach in Museology. In 1976, the international committee for education and culture, ICOM/CECA had further discussions on the new role of museums and gave momentum to the new movement. In this meeting the word ecomuseum had been coined as a more glamorous term for the integrated museum. The word ecomuseum was devised by Hugues de Varine for the use by French minister for environment. But it is clear that it was chosen as a term of convenience, driven by political expediency.

A consequence of the protest against and attempt to change established, stagnating, museum practice was the formation during the 1980's of an association of museum workers called the International Movement for New Museology (MINOM). The group consist of museologists who have joined together to explore ideas of 'new' museum as a democratic, educational institution in the service of society development (particularly at the local and regional level).

Baron (1987) specifies the thrust of New Museology as follows: "this new active or community Museology resolutely challenges the museum as an institution, the omnipotence and omniscience of the curators, the domination of the fine arts over all other disciplines, aesthetic pleasure as the essential criterion of an object's value, the absolute precedence of objects over life and the abiding nature of the history and values of an elite that turns to its profit the resources of the planet, the creativity of its inhabitants and taxes of its fellow citizens".

The first public pronouncement of this new concept was made by a group who met in London in 1983 at the General conference of ICOM. An international seminar was held in Oaxtepec, Mexico in 1984 on "territory Heritage- Community eco-Museum: man and his environment". The first international workshop on Eco- Museum and the New Museology was organized at Montréal, Canada in 1984, which ultimately led to the

"Quebec Declaration". The resentment and dissatisfaction expressed in ICOFOM soon developed into a movement. ICOFOM arranged a symposium in 1984 on the theme, "Museum territory- Society: New Practice" which further defined the concept of Ecomuseum. Yet, another international workshop on new mueology was organised by the international movement for a new Museology (MINOR) in Aragon, Spain in Oct, 1987. The conclusion of the workshop was that museum methodology should be based on social realities and on theories.

Declaration of Quebee Preamble (12 oct 1987)

1. That the international museum community be invited to acknowledge this movement and to incorporate ecomuseum and community, neighbourhood museums etc. into the museum typology
2. That all the efforts be made so that local initiatives in which these principles are applied may be recognized and aided by public authorities
3. That in this spirit and in order to bring about the full flowering of this Museology and to permit it to operate efficiently, be created in close collaboration with the permanent structure;
   - An international eco-museum, community museums, committee within ICOM
   - An international federation of new Museology which could be associated with ICOM and ICOMOS, and those whose provisional headquarters would be in Canada
4. That a temporary working group be formed whose initial mandates would be; the setting up to the proposed structures, and the application of a triennial programme of meetings and international collaboration.

International workshop on New Museology, Aragon, Spain (Oct 1987)

- "Many museums collect, conserve and exhibit, but they remain separated from the present economic, social and cultural context, avoiding the mission of participating in the development of the societies they serve.

- A New Museology is working to develop a sense of wholeness on the part of man for this world; to deal with the present human state of being disconnected from the physical and natural world, of being fragmented in our production and knowledge
- A New Museology in which the object and that which is man made have their only role that of providing information about what is human and alive
- A New Museology inextricably linked with an area and its population
- A New Museology which related the past to the present and which by its perception of the continuity of time, contributes to the development of both the individual and his society
- A New Museology which, based upon interdisciplinary considers equally all the products of humanity - be they artistic, religious, technological, domestic or linguistic as integral components of culture, together being a coherent statement of the relationships within a community and of a community with its environment
- A New Museology does not address itself only to passive and anonymous public but to a public who are active partners and practitioners, the developers of their future
- A New Museology in which the professionals aspire to continuous training: in which the methods that evolve with communication must be constantly re- evaluated and distributed
- A New Museology which has no other ambition than to serve the society of which it is part in order to provide society with a tool for useful reflection on its changes and its progress".

Deirdre C. Stam says, New Museology..

- Upholds the traditional emphasis upon the collection, preservation and use of objects for ultimate social benefits.
- Encourages improved understanding of the complex social environment in which museums operate;

- Points out the need to recognize sophistication in the demands of its audiences;
- Encourages flexibility in interpretation of museum objects;
- Calls for the use of modes of communication familiar to modern audiences;
- Advocates increased communication of information among all interested parties, including stagg, object makers and museum visitors;
- Specific increased coordination of functions, especially in collecting, displaying and interpreting museum objects;
- Calls for increased understanding of the implicit economic and political biases of museums.

  Stam also mentioned that museums must develop the following techniques for the future in new museological concerns -

  - New methods for attempting understanding of society and audience;
  - New ways of testing visitors needs and responses;
  - New organizational structures and management approaches to deal with new and dynamic functional relationships;
  - New ways to evaluate productivity;
  - New communication patterns;
  - New approaches to information management and utilization.

New Museums in India

The concept of New Museum is a very late introduction in India and very few contribution has been noticed in this regard. The tradition although started in India during 90's, but received full attention when a all India seminar on 'New Museology and Indian Museums' was organized in Bhopal during the All India Museums Association (MAI) Conference and accordingly a seminar was organized in Guwahati in the year 1988. The seminar was instrumental in the adoption and development of new Museology in India, considering the concepts, philosophy and practices of the exponents of the ecomuseology and new Museology in 1988. It included community participation, community initiatives, community ownership and conituous community support, desirability of identifying territory, concept of decentralization of works etc. which represent the major strength of this movement.

Guwahati Declaration on 'New Museology' (Bedekar, 1995:167-69)

Considering the changing demands on museums to care for and conserve heritage in its widest sense and to interpret it in ways which will make the heritage meaningful to the country.

Considering that, in the past, museums were concerned primarily with heritage without simultaneously relating it to the ongoing struggle for socio-economic development and progress,

Considering the concepts, the philosophy and the practices of the exponents of the ecomuseology or new museology as discussed in the seminar at Guwahati, 1988,

Considering the impetus in the so called new museology to socialize it, to ensure community participation, community initiatives, community ownership and continuous community support, desirability of identifying territory, concept of decentralization of works etc. which represent the major strength of the movement,

Considering world wide recognition of the many ecomuseum in different parts of the world since 1971 in the demonstration of the value and feasibility of the new concepts,

Considering that the name 'new museology' has been creating a gap or dualism between the exponents of the new movement and the rest of museum professions because of their apprehensions about the unity of the discipline of museology,

Considering that the kinds of impulses and actions which emnate from the new museology were and are in evidence in the work of many museums including those in India as discussed in detail in the conference 1988,

We hereby adopt

1. That the attention of international museum community be invited to the apparent confrontation between the new museology and the traditional museums which may divert the attention of museologists from the most urgent crucial problems of conservation and interpretation of world 'heritage' which is coming under growing threat.
2. that all possible efforts be made to recognize the value of the condition of the 'new museology'
3. that in addition to the basic research much needed new orientations to socialize smuseology be recognized and
   a. the ICOM's defintion of museums and museology be suitably revised so that the new museums and concepts be incorporated in the existing traditional museum and museology.
   b. The Indian concept of trusteeship as elaborated in the Gandhian philosophy be extended to the sphere of museums which are to be established, maintained and operated as trusts in the hands of representatives of the concerned communities for the value based museological work in the directions choose by each community itself.

With the Guwahati declaration a new group formed with the support of MAI and ICOM India chapter to critically examine and incorporate the best concepts of new museology in the contemporary concept of one universal museology to make its broad based and report to the ICOM General Conference in Netherlands 1989 as to how the international museum movement can became fully cohesive. Moreover the contemporary museums must be invited to open new channels of two-way communication with the various sections of the community so that they themselves participate and support museums to attain the self chosen goals of integrative conservation of heritage.

New Museum Terminology

In the study of new museum theory there are some specific terminologies which are essential in understanding the structure of this new museum concept. Some of the terminologies related to new museum have been discussed briefly.

Territory – It is not simply defined in geographical administrative terms, but rather as any whole unit where the inhabitants share a common way of life culture, occupation or traditional custom. Every museum Ecomuseum or not has a territory be it a national, regional or local museum. For the traditional museum it is the concept of geographical territory that helps the museum define its collection policy and target audience. A territory frequently equates with political boundaries and the sources of financial support. The Ecomuseum concept of territory is different, in that it can more readily step beyond the artificial boundaries imposed by authority and select territories on the basis of topography, dialect, architecture, history, economy or customs. It is therefore the nature of the concept of territory and not the size that enables a distinction to be made between the Ecomuseum and a traditional museum.

Community – People residing in one territory having same cultural identity, values, traditions and socio economic needs. People in a community can belong from various ethnicity, tribes and castes. Defining community is hugely complex, a constantly changing pattern of the tangible and in tangible.

Wasserman defines a community as "a population living in an area, conscious of the affinities and the differences which characterize its elements, as well as the conflicting relationships between these and their environment and to whom at least the future is common. A community may be of various dimensions: village, country, region, nation, company, country, religious grouping, academic, immigrant, professional, family. Everybody belongs to a community, while at the same time crossing several others: an individual chooses certain communities, while others are imposed on him by law, events or birth."

Collective Memory : Transgenerational knowledge accumulated and developed by the indigenous people and groups relating to the properties, uses and characteristics of the biological diversity. A significant feature of collective memory that with every generation it accumulates new features and so it has an ever changing dimension.

Heritage : It is to be understood in terms of the universal expression of inheritance. French equivalent of the word heritage is the 'patrimony' which stands for the cultural properties handed down from generation to generation. As a matter of fact heritage, as it is stands for continuity in time and space.

Heritage is the sum total of wild life and scenic parks, sites of scientific and historical importance, national monuments, historic monuments, works of art literature and music, oral traditions and museum collections and their documentation which provides the basis for a shared culture and creativity in the arts.(South African Governments White Paper on Arts Culture and Heritage,1996)

As per Cowenthal (1997) "heritage plays an essential role in husbanding community, identity, distinction in between history and heritage declaring that 'history explores and explains pasts grown ever more opaque over time, heritage clarifies pasts so as to infuse them with present purpose'."

Is an expression of the ways of living developed by a community and passed on from generation to generation including customs, practices, places, objects, artistic expressions and values. Cultural heritage is often expressed as either Intangible or Tangible cultural heritage. (ICOMOS, ICTC, 2002)

Tangible heritage : Heritage is an integrated man made space- the tangible part of which is built in, concrete, visible and unchangeable that manifests in movable and immovable forms.

Intangible heritage : According to Oxford dictionary intangible means, not tangible; incapable of being perceived by the sense of touch, as incorporeal or immaterial things; impalpable; not definite or clear to the mind; intangible arguments; (of an asset) existing only in connection with something else, as the goodwill of a business; something intangible.esp. an intangible asset; Intangibles are hard to value.

Beyond the much celebrated and highly explored space of the tangible forms there lie a misty, short lived but vibrant space in the realm of human heritage, which evades every sense except sight and sound. The space is limitless and ageless and in many ways responsible for the creations, recreations and propagations of the various tangible cultural properties from time immemorial. The intangible cultural heritage embrace all forms of traditional, popular or folk culture i.e. collective works originating in a given community and based on tradition. These creations are transmitted orally or by gesture, and are modified over a period of time through a process of collective recreation.

There is a symbiotic relationship between the tangible and the intangible. The intangible heritage should be regarded as the larger framework within which tangible heritage takes shape and significance.

The tangible cultural heritage, be it a monument a historic city or a landscape, takes on shape and significance, is easy to catalogue and its protection consists mainly of conservation and restoration measures. Intangible heritage, on the other hand, consists of processes and practices and accordingly requires a different safeguarding approach and methodology to the tangible heritage. It is fragile by its very nature and therefore much more vulnerable than other forms of heritage. Safeguarding the intangible heritage involves the collection, documentation and archiving of cultural property and the protection and support of its bearers. While the tangible cultural heritage is designed to outlive those who produce or commission it, the fate of the intangible heritage is far more intimately related to its creators as it depends in most cases on oral transmission. Therefore, the legal and administrative measures traditionally taken to protect material elements of cultural heritage are in most cases inappropriate for safeguarding a heritage whose most significant elements relate to particular systems of knowledge.

Cultural Mapping : It is the documentation of both tangible and intangible heritage of the area. Cultural mapping enables us to understand and share culture; to re-think history; and to promote creativity and development. This toolkit focuses primarily on promoting creativity and development. Where cultural mapping can be most valuable is in generating new perspectives and preparing the ground for effective cultural planning.

Cultural mapping is a valuable tool for identifying a community's strength and its resources. Cultural mapping creates tools to make the least possible use of those resources and assets.

Traditional Knowledge : An understanding of traditional knowledge and how it differs from non-indigenous knowledge is an important basis for determining how to use it. Knowing what it contains and how it is acquired and held is fundamental to being able to make good use of the knowledge and to encourage all parties to be aware of the added value its use will bring.

The Director General of United Nations Educational, Scientific and Cultural Organization defines traditional knowledge as:

The indigenous people of the world possess an immense knowledge of their environments, based on centuries of living close to nature. Living in and from the richness and variety of complex ecosystems, they have an understanding of the properties of plants and animals, the functioning of ecosystems and the techniques for using and managing them that is particular and often detailed. In rural communities in developing countries, locally occurring species are relied on for many - sometimes all - foods, medicines, fuel, building materials and other products. Equally, people are knowledge and perceptions of the environment, and their relationships with it, are often important elements of cultural identity.

Most indigenous people have traditional songs, stories, legends, dreams, methods and practices as means of transmitting specific human elements of traditional knowledge. Sometimes it is preserved in artifacts handed from father to son or mother to daughter. In indigenous knowledge systems, there is usually no real separation between secular and sacred knowledge and practice - they are one and the same. In virtually all of these systems, knowledge is transmitted directly from individual to individual.

In any event, knowledge leads us to understand the significance of tradition. Over the centuries, local traditions have developed valuable experience, techniques for protecting the environment and skills for handling social conflict (drama, games, customs, rites, and folk healing skills, to mention but a few), which make up a treasure trove of common knowledge for mankind. It is no accident that exactly ten years have passed since UNESCO accepted the *Recommendation on the Safeguarding of Traditional Culture and Folklore*.

Culture : Dynamic totality of distinctive spiritual, material, intellectual and emotional features which characterize a society or social group. It includes – the arts and letters, as also modes of life, the fundamental rights of the human being, value systems, and traditions, heritage beliefs developed over time and subject to change. (South African Governments white paper on Arts, Culture & Heritage, 1996)

The system of shared beliefs, values, customs, behaviours and artefacts that the members of the society use to cope with their world and with one another and that are transmitted from generation to generation through learning.

Culture is a socially acquired phenomenon. It engulfs Tangible objects and Intangible codes developed and used by man in a total environment for the purpose of sustaining, supporting and improving life. Its intangible manifestations are institutions, thought processes, philosophy value systems and social codes. The tangible manifestations can be broadly classified into built heritage like the monuments & historic sites and movable heritage such as the antiquities and artefacts.

Culture encompasses the diverse creative activities in material & spiritual domains (literature, visual and performing arts and various forms of artistic expressions) which provide material sustenance give a sense of purpose to human existence. It provides the reflective poise, aesthetic fulfillment and the moral, ethical/ spiritual energy so essential for the growth & development of a good healthy society. (Ministry of Culture, Government of India).

Cultural Identity : It is a treasure that sensitizes mankind's possibilities of self fulfillment by moving every people and every group to seek, to nurture in its past, and to welcome contributions from outside that are compatible with its own characteristics and to continue the process of its own creation. All cultures form part of the common heritage of mankind. The cultural identity of a people is renewed and enriched through contact with the traditions and values of others. Culture is a dialogue, the exchange of ideas and experience and the appreciation of other values and traditions; it emerges from the experience of all worlds' people as each affirms its own identity. Local identity or cultural identity is a character which makes areas remarkable and coherent so that they serve as a basis for pride, affection and a sense of continuity

It is the duty of international community to ensure that the culture and cultural identity of each people is preserved and protected. The neglect or destruction of the culture of any group is a loss to mankind as a whole. New museum theory therefore strives to help different people to trace their cultural identity.

Material Culture : It is the study of human made physical objects or artefacts in social settings to understand the beliefs, values, ideas, attitudes and assumptions of a particular community or society at a given time. It enables us to understand the meanings of the texts and to highlight the social and cultural history embedded in them.

The study of material culture includes the analysis of a spectrum of objects- from the use of space to something as simple as a teapot, photograph or a chair in one's home.

Material culture in this respect can be described as an object based branch of cultural history. It allows us to give voice to the voiceless; it enables us to see objects as a form of visual literacy that can be read. It differs from archaeology in that many archaeologists disengage from the study of beliefs. The province of cultural anthropology and even more from aesthetics, the province of art history.

Oral History : It can be defined as the recording, preservation and interpretation of historical information, based on the personal experiences and opinions of the speaker.

It often takes the form of eye-witness evidence about past events, but can include folklore, myths, songs and stories passed down over the years by word of mouth. While it is an invaluable way of preserving the knowledge and understanding of older people, it can also involve interviewing younger generations. More recently, the use of video recording techniques has expanded the realm of oral history beyond verbal forms of communication and into the realm of gesture.

- Oral history is the recording of people's memories. It is the living history of everyone's unique life experiences.
- Oral history records people's experiences on sound and video tape. It is a vital tool for our understanding of the recent past. No longer are we dependent only on the written word.
- Oral history enables people who have been hidden from history to be heard, and for those interested in their past to record personal experiences and those of their families and communities.
- Oral history is new and exciting because it is interactive: it is shared history and a rare chance to actually talk to history face to face.
- Oral history preserves everyone's past for the future.

In-situ Preservation : The principle of the preservation In situ is a very modern one and in keeping with the latest developments in the presentation of cultural heritage. In situ preservation is an important characteristic of the Ecomuseum. In situ preservation encompasses the whole territory in a broad manner, involving culture, history and local traditions aiding their preservation and dissemination since they represent the roots of the community. Ecomuseum is the only mechanism which preserves and interprets heritage In situ rather than divorce it from its location as occurs with traditional museum. Interpretation should be site based demonstrating the significance of the place and conservation.

Contextualization : In terms of museum it means relating the object to its context or surroundings. The object acquires its complete meaning when it is placed in its original surroundings. In Ecomuseum In situ preservation of objects take place. This provides the scope for a holistic interpretation of the object.

Decontextualization : Museum collect their original material from natural, social and cultural environments. Those are preserved, documented, researched into and exhibited in the public galleries. The individual specimen of nature and objects of arts and crafts get separated from their original environment or contexed. This is decontextualization. For e.g.- a drum belonging to a tribal village if taken and displayed in a museum gallery loses its original context in the new surroundings. Thus the drum is decontextualised.

Museums based on New Museum theory

The function and structure of the above types of new museums are mostly similar with many areas overlapping. Only few key principles classify them into different heads.

Neighbourhood Museum

Although officially the establishment of museums based on the principles of new museum started after the UNESCOs Santiago (1972) and Quebec (1984) General conferences, where Hugh de Varine and Rivere coined the word ecomuseum and its concept. It led to the establishment of many ecomuseums in Europe. But the process of community service through museums had already started in the world as evident from the neighbourhood museum of Anacostia established way back in 1967.

The term neighbourhood in its strict geographical sense relates to an area within the periphery around a museum. The concept of Neighbourhood museum first developed in America. Due to unchecked, unplanned growth of the suburbs and migration of rural population to urban areas in search of better avenues in life there grew dwelling pockets in the fringes of cities whose inhabitants faced grappling problems of racism, material disparity, poverty, poor housing, drug menace and education etc. It is here the concept of Neighbourhood museum was found to be of great help in working as an intermediary between city museum and community.

The Anacostia Neighbourhood museum was an extension of the Smithsonian Institute and was established in 1967. It was selected because it represented all the urban ills existing in the modern cities of America. In the Neighbourhood museum, the people of the community speak and the museum listens to them. The Neighbourhood museum starts collecting data, analyzing and studying that by posing problems together with alternative solutions.

Ecomuseum

The new trends in museum development and the role of the community to preserve and promote its cultural and natural heritage led to the establishment of ecomuseum. Ecomuseum is often confused with New Museology. New Museology is the theory and it is a much wider phenomenon, while Ecomuseum is a part of the bigger umbrella called new museums. (Details discussed in later chapters).

Village Museum

Similar to ecomuseum, village museum presents a set of sites within the territory grouped together to form a highly contextualized environment. By its very nature, it is suitable for staging live activities. The percentage of local visitors is generally not very high and the majority is tourists. But this type of museum lends itself to the use of reconstructed buildings and extras in a form representation sometime closer to that of open- air museums, interpretation centers or theme parks than to that of ecomuseum. These types of village museums, which are not defined as ecomuseum but develop the integrated conservation of heritage, have been carried forward in Great Britain at Beamish, Iron Bridge Gorge and Glastonbury.

Community Museum

Radical changes brought about by modern world is being transplanted over the culture of the developing countries. This onslaught is destroying the social structures, social institutions, indigenous arts and crafts. The so called developmental plans and strategies often fail because the local people are not included in decision making process. To face these problems new model of Museology has developed. The new model called the community museum developed as an integral part of the community development project. The mutual understanding, co- operation and active participation of the people in the community development programmes are the corner- stone of the concept of community museum. These museums are primarily a political instrument in mobilizing the masses. The people in general have to investigate their own cultural traditions. The concept was first developed at a local level at Tanzania in accordance with their hereditary tradition. Ujamma village in Tanzania presented the first and foremost an experiment in establishing a community museum. Community museum gives more emphasis on research, to know the past and present of the community and their cultural ethnography. Apart from history, it covers the areas of political science, economics, religion and so on. Thus it provides better foundations which will help in the development of the new cultural identity. In India the Korlai community museum was developed by V.H Bedekar.

Thus, the concept of folk culture is very vital to the museological activities in the form of community museums.

Integral Museum

The concept of integral museum implies that the museum opens up its field and traditional domain for a full realization of Anthropological, socio- economic and technological development. An integral museum has its starting point in the public and not in the objects. The museum is established only if the people want it and in the way they want to function to serve the socio economic and cultural needs of the society. Such museums are more suited for small and medium sized population. The integrated museum is not related to single discipline but it takes an overall view and integrated approach to the existing problems of the society and integrated treatment by the active participation of all sections of the society. For this purpose, the integral museum requires the permanent or temporary assistance of experts from various disciplines, including the social science. It is said that while concept of eco museum is of European origin, the concept of integral museum has emerged in Latin America. Barquisimeto museum in Venezuela is an example of integral museum. The basic aim of the museum was to make the community to know all about their local heritage and also plan their own development.

Living History Museum

The concept of Living History Museum has grown out of an older living history Farm movement which was started in late seventies. The association for living historical Farms and agriculture museum was started at the Farmer's museum in co-opers town, New York. Since then the concept of living history has been influencing the role of history museum in North America.

Initially, it was Darwin Kelsey, in early seventies at old Sturbridege village in Eastern Massachusetts along with a group of coworkers set up the first well researched living history Farm presenting the life of a typical family of the areas in 1830s. According to Darwin Kilsey, the Farms were iconic models and they could and should be designed to present physical realties in one or several appropriate scales.

Since then, the living history Farm movement has developed into a much bigger and broader living history movement in North America. It included historic sites such as Clayville near Springfield, Illinois, operated by the University, Sangamon State. The movement further included transformed Open Air Museum, such as the corner prairie Pioneer Settlement, North of Indianapolis, Indiana. Here, costumed interpreters speak as if they were actual residents of the community in 1830s and represent people of different regional cultural backgrounds, as well as occupations and social classes.

Living history programme and facilities are designed by the conceptions of the typical or particular model of the "scaled representation." Interdisciplinary research on local social history, folk-life studies and cultural geography is emphasized. There is more interest on the spoken word and objects in an appropriate setting and what they objectively communicate to people.

Thus, the Museology of the living history movement is not a discipline but interdisciplines, just as environmental studies. As regards to the functions of a Living History Museum, they are akin to any other museum. For example, the Living History Museums collect and preserve such objects which represent life in the household, Farmstead, field, workshop or public building.

Accurate reproductions based on objects of document research are much preferred. They are known as 'analogous objects'. Utensils of the kitchen, tools of the garden and workshop fall within this category. Even the fields, the fences, the plantings and the buildings assembled to represent an actual cultural landscape are viewed as macro artifacts and treated as artifacts in the collection. This gives an idea of in situ preservation.

Research is the extremely important function for Living History Museums. The appropriate tools, utensils and implements for time and place must be discovered in documentary sources, examples located, if possible, and reproduced. It may also use census-records, tax and deed records, Farm account books and local maps etc.

Exhibition is another significant function for Living History Museums. The interpretive planning as they call it, translates the research into a physical setting. The Living History Museums are therefore, different than the theme parks which are meant only to entertain people.

References

Bedekar, V.H., *New Museology for India*, New Delhi, 1995.

Varine, H.de, *Ecomuseums or community museums? 25 years of applied research in Museology and Development*, Nordisk Museologi, 1996.

Chapter 3

Ecomuseum

The Concept

The concept of ecomuseum evolved in France in the late 1960's and has since been adopted as a new form of museum throughout Europe as well as Brazil, Canada and Australia. Ecomuseum concept embraces all aspects of cultural and natural heritage, including sites, objects, buildings and natural endowments in the form of significant landscapes, flora and fauna and the intangible properties like performing arts, oral traditions and folklore. The functioning of ecomuseum takes place within a defined geographical area or territory. Central to the ecomuseum ideal is the intimate association of local communities in the process of caring for their heritage. Providing local people with an opportunity to conserve and exhibit the significant nature or aspects of territory and the life style. Traditional museum face many problems when attempting to encapsulate the significant identity of a place and living tradition of the local communities. The traditional museum deals with history of human culture and environment in a static way and not the living culture and by conservation and upgradation. Hence, ecomuseum philosophy and practice has provided a means of overcoming the limits of the traditional museums.

Territory is a significant term in the context of ecomuseum, being an important facet of both philosophy and practice. Territory is not only an indication of the geographical limits of the ecomuseum but also engulfs everything within its jurisdiction. Consequently the 'eco' in ecomuseums demands considerable flexibility – it is both space and time and interconnections.

The term ecomuseum has been evolved during the growing concern about environment in 70's. Natural environment initially played a pivotal role in the ecomuseum movement. Later on not only the natural environment, but also it focused its concern about the man made environment. Ecomuseums are the museums of time as well museums of space. A given environment allows human being to link with time and space. This is specially significant to ecomuseums. Consequently, an unique timeless component of environment such as a river, a sacred groove etc. are also significant in the realm of eco museum. Besides, tangible cultural materials that are left behind by our ancestors such as archaeological monuments, ancient art objects and inscriptions etc. – the built environment that of the past are equally significant. In other words, ecomuseums serve to conserve and interpret all the elements of the environment mentioned above in order to establish the continuity with the past and a sense of belonging.

To understand ecomuseum it is essential to explore concept of 'cultural identity' and 'community', as they both relate to museums in general. UNESCO (Viet, 1980:498) defines 'cultural identity' as the correspondence between a community (national, ethnic, linguistic etc.) and its cultural life, as well as the right of each community to its own culture.

Definitions

Georges Henry Riviere defined and redefined ecomuseum three times. His final definition published in 1980 as follows :

> 'an instrument conceived, fashioned and operated jointly by a public authority and its local population. The public authority's involvement is through the experts, facilities and resources it provides; the local population's involvement depends on its aspirations, knowledge and individual approach. It is a mirror in which the local population views itself to discover its own image, in which it seeks an explanation of the territory to which it is attached and of the populations which have preceded it, seen either as circumscribed in time or in terms of the continuity of generations. It is a mirror that the local population holds up to its visitors so that it may be better understood and so that its industry, customs and identity may command respect. It is an expression of man and nature. It situates man in his natural environment. It portrays nature in its wilderness, but also as adapted by traditional and industrial society in their own image. It is an expression of time, when the explanations it offers reach back before appearance of man, ascend the course of the prehistoric and historical times in which he lived and arrive finally at man's present. It also offers a vista of the future, while having no pretensions of decision making, its function being rather to inform and critically analyze. It is an interpretation of space, of special places in which to stop and stroll. It is a laboratory in so far as it contributes to the study of the past and present of the population concerned and of its total environment and promotes the training of specialists in these fields, in co-operation with outside research bodies. It is a conservation center, in so far as it helps to preserve and develop the natural and cultural

heritage of the population. It is a school, in so far as it involves the population in its work of study and protection and encourages it to have clearer grasp of its own future. This laboratory conservation center and school are based on common principles. The culture in the name of which they exist is to be understood in its broadest sense and they are concerned to foster awareness of its dignity and artistic manifestation from whatever stratum of the population they derive. Its diversity is limitless, so greatly to its elements vary from one specimen to another. This triad is not self-enclosed; it gives and it receives'.

Riviera's definition includes many significant concepts such as community, territory, landscape, local identity, a sense of history which are important in creating a sense of belonging. The most important feature of Riviera's definition is the repetition of the word 'population' in relation to the idea of ecomuseum having 'limitless diversity' – a suggestion that the ecomuseum can be anything local people and museum professionals want it to be. Another important feature of his definition, according to Peter Davis (Davis 1999: 68) is 'it is an interpretation of space – of special places in which to stop and stroll'. This suggests that the ecomuseum is not limited to a building or even a open-air site, but everything within the demarcated region it refers to as its 'territory'. Within the designated area are cultural and ecological elements that have special meaning and are integrated in the eco museum. There might be natural features, a historical site or examples of vernacular architecture, religion or traditional industrial structure. Riviera's definition does not incorporate anything about the traditional museum activities like collection, documentation, other than it helps to preserve and develop the natural and cultural heritage of the population. We must assume that heritage is more than just material culture, encompassing intangible elements like memories, folklore, music, dance and song. In general the ecomuseum includes everything within its territory. Local skills, behaviour patterns, social structure and traditions are as much a part of the ecomuseum as the tangible evidence of natural landscapes, unique geological features, wildlife, buildings and objects, people and their domestic animals.

Corsane and Holleman (1993:111-25) suggest that the ecomuseum incorporates a much larger territory in a fairly open ended manner. Here, the territory is not simply defined in a geographical or administrative term, but rather as any whole unit where the inhabitants share a common way of life, culture and heritage co-ordinated from a kind of headquarter. The ecomuseum could have series of 'antennae' within the territory. These antennae form a network through which the activities of information gathering, research, display and education can be performed. For the visitors, the antennae which are scattered within the territory are generally linked by traditional roads connecting various scenic spots. The idea of ecomuseum being a network of sites has resulted in the use of the term 'fragmented museum'. It is this aspect of the concept that resulted in 'museolization' of heritage sites as noticed in the recently founded ecomuseums (Davis 1999:68).

There have been many other attempts to state succinctly what is an ecomuseum how it could be distinguished from the traditional museum. The Natural History Committee of ICOM was evidently concerned by the adoption of the term (Anon, 1978:2-4). The naturists felt that the term could seemingly be applied in a variety of circumstances, however it had deviated from its original 'ecological' context. As a consequence the committee suggested the following definition –

> 'the ecomuseum is an institution which manages, studies and exploits by scientific, educational and generally speaking, cultural means, the entire heritage of a given community, including the whole natural environment and cultural milieu. Thus the ecomuseum is a vehicle for public participation in community planning and development. To this end, the ecomuseum uses all means and methods at its disposal in order to allow the public to comprehend, criticize and master – in a liberal and responsible manner – the problems, which it faces. Essentially the ecomuseum uses the language of the artifact, the reality of everyday life and concrete situations in order to achieve desired changes'.

Rene Rivard has provided the most useful definition by comparing the traditional museum (building + collection + experts +public) to the ecomuseum (territory + heritage + memory + population). She also makes a distinction between traditional 'museum of ecology' (= natural history museums), ecological museums (= field centers, interpretive sites, natural parks and natural reserves) and ecomuseums (Rivard 1988: 123-28). She suggests that the latter address specially the interactions between humans and the natural environment and involve the community in creating and 'improving' the environment by helping to conserve traditional habitats and eco systems. Whether these distinctions are valid and whether ecomuseums can play a conservation role, is open to debate. Furthermore, Rivard identifies four categories of ecomuseums –

1. the discovery ecomuseum (the traditional and first holistic model)
2. the development ecomuseum (concerned with the community, cultural identity, economic regeneration and with stated political goals)
3. specialist ecomuseums (dealing with specific industries) and
4. 'combat' ecomuseums (usually in urban locations and dedicated to pressing social issues).

After Riviere, Hugues de Varine opines that ecomuseum should not go for a conventional collecting policy, because objects must preferably be left on site, where they can be interpreted in the context. It is interesting to note that in his retrospective assessment of the ecomuseum, de Varine reduces the objectives of the ecomuseum to four key points, but using some of the key words from Riviera's definition.

1. as an object and data bank for the community
2. to serve as an observatory of change (and to help the community react to changes)
3. to become a laboratory – a focal point for meetings, discussion and new initiatives

4. to be a showcase – revealing the community and its habitat to visitors.

This is not a definition as such but it does provide a useful indication after some 20 years of experimentation of what an ecomuseum might realistically achieve.

The official definition of the ecomuseum is now enshrined in French statute as the Ecomuseum Charter which was granted on the instructions of the Ministry of Culture and Communication on the 4th March 1981. The essential feature of this definition is the significance of community involvement.

Characteristics features

Following are some of the characteristics features of ecomuseums (Bedekar, 1995:34-49)

1. Collection of objects does not play central role in ecomuseums. Here objects are not sacred, excessively glorified or almost sanctified. The fact of humanism is the underlying factor of eco museums.

2. Eco museum operates on the premise that people have a right to know their heritage and also right to use it appropriately and for their own well being. Eco museum gives priority to persuading people to identify their heritage, use it to reaffirm their identity. The groups of people should not be embarrassed to proclaim their group identities as wholesome activity. It lays special stress on the use of heritage for identity building exercise. Museum is an institutionalized access to people's heritage.

3. Right to heritage – this concept has been made meaningful by ecomuseums with an organized initiation, guidance, instruction and education followed by close familiarity with actual material.

4. Ecomuseums consider it their reason for existence to help people learn about their heritage. But as they differ in their interests and capacity to learn, the people will have to be actively involved in the learning process. Passive learning has no place in non-conventional museums in which they are not treated as outsiders.

5. Ecomuseums make possibility of intimate knowledge linked up free and repeated access to cultural material which is not always available in the conventional museums at users convenience.

6. Eco museums enable people to know their heritage by inviting them to become involved in museum work.

7. In eco museums the collective memory is a key concept. It is this collective memory, which constitutes heritage of an individual who has shown readiness to identify with a group.

8. Eco museology has its main focus in people and not on objects.

9. Eco museums have no place for social passivity of the usual museum visitors or onlookers. Pursuit of action and creative work are encouraged in the eco museums so that people do not remain passive and stagnant.

10. Eco museology is nothing if it is not involved actively in the community development. Heritage is treated firstly as the resource for the purpose of community development. Heritage, therefore, is not isolated from its social context of the past, present and even future.

11. Ecomuseum holds that a museum can not be confined to a building. A museum can be anywhere and everywhere within a specified territory.

12. Ecomuseum does not believe in over specialization of research and interpretation. The emphasis is on holistic or interdisciplinary approach.

13. Since museology is to be practiced by the common man and it is used by them for their participation, the role of the public is that of participants in several ways as decision makers, as volunteers, as media men, public relation people, technicians, guides, demonstrator, interpreters etc.

14. A conventional museum organize its collections according to the dictate of the academic disciplines. Academic standards are decisive in museum presentation and interpretation including research. The museum experts are more concerned about their accomplishments as individual professionals. It is exclusively concerned about the 'collective' success of the institution and participating public in the protection and interpretation of their heritage.

15. Ecomuseums do not consider museums and objects acquired by them as ends in themselves. Conventional museum appear to do so in its obession with perpetuating the traditional relationship between the society and museum collections.

16. Communication in the conventional museum is essentially one way. In eco museums one way communication is scrupulously avoided by encouraging and insisting on interactive programmes.

17. In ecomuseums the forms and contents of communication are not decided by the professionals. The agents of dissemination are also lay people but well informed about what they communicate in relation to the museum situation. Heritage specially can be interpreted most, vivdly by those who are part of it. Even the most complex aspects of such heritage can be explained authoritatively by the interpreters

on behalf of ecomuseums, because they are insiders directly involved and because they are close witnesses of traditions and cultures of the territory. Moreover they are familiar with the languages or dialects of common people who form the majority of users of ecomuseums.

18. Eco museums aim at being as open as possible institutionally to fulfill the contemporary ideal of democratization of all social institutions.

19. Eco museums believe in the development of people because of the realization that in the post industrial period, people will be more selective and discriminating in what they choose to do themselves and to further their social interests, talents and identity. Here the concept of 'demasification' assumes special significance.

20. Eco museums aspire to transform the process of heritage maintenance into a collective social enterprise. The basis for this is the new museological principle that museums deal with memory of a society and not with objects torn out of the context of such memory. Therefore, the new ideal is not to satisfy specialist professionals who work in museums, who often pursue personal interests and goals or who enjoy communicating primarily with like minded people.

21. Eco museum tends to decontrol institutional definition of relationship between objects and the people. Conventional exhibits tends to create artificial and stereotyped contexts.

22. Ecomuseums take equal interest both in material and non-material culture. Recording of folk-lore and reminiscence are held very useful form of oral culture. Conventional museums are biased towards acquiring three dimensional objects and specimens of material culture. Yet, as experts

tell us, identity is very often found in non- material cultural heritage.

23. Ecomuseums do not give utmost priority to the task of saving individual objects of living crafts because of the conviction that if craftsman survives then the crafts will survive and then the traditions will survive. Heritage must survive so that customs will survive and the craftsman will get necessary patronage to survive because many traditional crafts are connected with local customs and rituals.

24. Ecomuseums try to select people from the public who are willing to serve the museum voluntarily. Then they are trained in the professional area of museography as well as in the basic philosophy of New Museology.

25. Ecomuseums encourage individuals to identify themselves with their environment consciously. This prevents the opposite process of alienation from a persons own cultural milieu.

26. Ecomuseums do not consider themselves as museums of certain kinds of material like Fine Arts material, crafts, dresses and costumes, gems and jewellery. So the ecomuseums do not give high priority to the task of making people visit museums to see objects as is done in the conventional museums. Here approach is different. The museum is for the people and people forms the museum. Objects are provided for the meaningful awareness of the heritage, of a community. Museum is not objects but of the activity of the people. It is the community to which ecomuseum is committed not collections.

27. Ecomuseums establish permanent contacts with local university, learned bodies and educational, scientific and cultural institutions and centers not as an after-thought but

as preparatory or pre-requisite to offer their services. These relations are for mutual co- operation.

28. Ecomuseums are very particular about the study and illustration of local economic and industrial activities and they tend to serve as bridge between the public, the workers and the industrialists.

29. Ecomuseums allow a long period of gestation of the project. In this an extensive programme is carried out. It consists of study visits, field works, documentation, survey, seminars, even exhibitions for the local people till they are convinced of the utility of the new museum.

30. Ecomuseums undertake study of local crafts and revive them if threatened. New museums attempt to make such occupations viable so that the craftsmen can live with dignity and not on charities.

Growth and Development of Ecomuseum

The development of the concept of ecomuseum is regarded as 'heritage movement', which emerged during the last quarter of the 20th cent. The movement evolved throughout the world specially in the 'developed world' and it had a remarkable impact on museums, not only that it prompted new approaches to exhibition but also to a new kind of museum.

Lets have quick look into the foundation of this movement. People have been making museums for several hundred years and the early history of museums is closely associated with a growing interest in the natural environment. Making collection of animals, plants and fossils in order to try and understand the diversity of nature was an established practice during the Renaissance. In a world being explored and exploited, there was little scope of a conservation role for museums, the practice was to amass as many objects as possible. Only by doing so, natural history museum and natural history curators carried out taxonomic research like identifying, naming and classifying animals and plants – both recent and extinct and present a complete picture of the world to museum visitors. The basic work carried out in natural history museum altered very little during the later years of the 19th cent. And during early 20th cent,- collecting, cataloguing and curating specimens was essentially directed towards a better understanding of the taxonomy of animals and plants. Although new method in presenting nature had been made – specially the use of diorama depicting the interactions between species and the habitat as a visual panoramic description. Most of the natural history museums continued to present nature as an ordered series of specimens, both zoological and botanical. Albert Parr, Director of the American Museum of Natural History from 1942 – 1959, was arguably the first museologist to contemplate a new role for natural history museums. Parr realized that if museums were going to remain pertinent to society then they had to reorient themselves and take up new challenges (Davis, 1999:7). One of the most significant test facing museums was to respond to the emergence of a growing concern for the natural environment, in the later part of 20th cent.

The 1960 was a decade of unparalleled catastrophe, with spectacular and disastrous oil spills and discovery of the impact of organoclorine pesticides on the environment and its bad effect on animals. It was also a time that saw popular protest emerging as a powerful vehicle for the protection of the natural and human heritage.

The environmental movement had made its mark on natural history museums; they had identified their urgent and vital purposes. Parallel to environmental concern and the new role of natural history museums there was a call for review of the role of all museums in response to other new concerns. Both the movements demanded museums to be more responsive to the needs of society and to step out beyond the comfort zone demarcated by buildings and collections. Peter Van Mensch has labeled this phenomenon as 'the second museum revolution' (Davis, 1999: 9). As part of this revolution during 1960's some traditional museums began to modify long established philosophies and practices in order to relate to societal needs. As a result different types of museums began to be founded often at a local level in order to save fragments of heritage and to make a statement about local identity. The changes in museum practice and the establishment of new museums took place at a time of considerable societal turmoil, resultant changes in society were accompanied by radical changes in thinking about the nature and purpose of museums. The ecomuseum with its strong emphasis on community involvement demands action by the community to conserve its own material culture and natural heritage within the boundaries of its geographical area or territory was one of the proposed new approaches. It became a focal point for debate about the purpose of museums.

The evolution of ecomuseums has been a continuous process. Although the ideas that lay behind the foundation of the first ecomuseums were innovative, they are closely linked to and influenced by earlier museum models. New and radical ideas had begun to emerge before the later part of 20th cent. and many of these including the heimatmuseum, the open air museum, folklife museum and neighbourhood museums had a considerable influence on the museologists involved in understanding history of the ecomuseum.

The ideology of second museum revolution lead to the reassessment of both theoretical and practical aspects of museums with imaginative ideas permeating all museum functions. The other aspect of change – museums in the service of the society, communities and their development were voiced strongly at the General Assemblies of ICOM. They surface first at the 9th meeting in Munich in August 1968. the first resolution agreed by this meeting was that 'museums be recognized as major institutions in the service of development' because of the contribution they can make to cultural, social and economic life. The 10th meeting that held in Grenoble in 1971 urged museums to 'undertake a continuous and complete assessment of the needs of the public which they serve' and 'evolve methods of action which will in future more firmly establish their educational and cultural roles in the service of mankind'. The first resolution included following points:

- That the museum must accept the fact that society is constantly changing.
- That the traditional concept of the museum which perpetuates values concerned with the preservation of man's cultural and natural heritage not as a manifestation of all that is significant in man's development, but merely as the possession of objects is questionable.
- That each individual museum must accept that it has a duty to evolve means of action specially designed to serve best the particular social environment in which it operates.
- That the museum visiting public is not necessarily the total public which the museum should be serving.
- That museums have not taken advantage of the wide range of expertise and knowledge which exists in other sections of the community.

Following the resolutions agreed in Grenoble, in the UNESCO-ICOM round table meeting held in Santiago from 20th May to 31st May 1972, community involvement remain the key point. Here, museums professionals and other specialists discussed the role of museums in relation to the social and economic needs of modern day society in Latin America. Four key themes had been identified beforehand for discussion, namely,

- Museums and cultural development in the rural environment and the development of agriculture.
- Museums and social and cultural problems of the environment
- Museums and scientific and technological development.
- Museums and life long education.

By the Santiago meeting, a new term 'integrated museum' developed. It was this concept that formed the cornerstone of the resolutions passed in Santiago and published by UNESCO in 'Museums' in 1973.Although these radical ideas were initially ignored even passing unnoticed by the museum at large at the time, the Santiago meeting can be identified as one of the turning point in museological thought.

De Varine and his colleague Georges Henri Riviera were central to the development of the new ideas to the museums, including the ecomuseum. Riviere steeped in the traditions of French ethnography, was anxious to interpret human history and the objects and artifacts associated with that history in an environmental context. De Varine deeply committed to the democratization of museums, wished to promote the community role of museums within an economic and political framework. Although the word 'ecomuseum' was first utilized in 1971, it is widely argued that, Riviere laid the foundations of the ecomuseum movement a quarter of a century earlier in planning the Bretagne Museum in Rennes (Boylan, 1992: 29). This had occurred in 1947, in 1953 when Riviere planned an exhibition in Gennevilliers, enlisting the help of local people. There can be little doubt that Riviera's deep involvement with French ethnography, the way in which his approaches to interpretation had changed and the realization that traditional ways of life were being threatened were all significant triggers for the ecomuseum movement.

The late 1960's and early 1970 saw the testing of the theories that Riviere and de Varine had proposed, specially in France and French speaking Canada. The ecomuseum emerged in two very different guises, the first (the discovery museum) based on ecological principles and closely allied to the nature reserve movement in France, the second more closely geared to the needs of communities (development or community ecomuseums).

The Ecomuseum Models

The Canadian museologist, Pierre Mayrand, when setting up the ecomuseum of Haute-Beauce in Qubec, expressed the process in the form of a 'creativity triangle' which shows the ecomuseum developing as a result of interpretive activities within its geographical area. An interpretation center lies at the apex, which increases public awareness of the geographical area or territory through its activities, which would include the creation of antennae. Myrand has subsequently refined his 'creativity triangle' and placed it within a theoretical 'three year cycle', the implication is that within three years it is possible to move from idea to foundation, from apathy to empathy and to pass through transitional stages of museology which he identifies as pre-museology, para-museology, museology, post-museology and trans-museology.

Rene Rivard's definition of the ecomuseum alluded to earlier is most easily understood, specially when presented graphically. Rivard makes a direct contrast between the traditional and ecomuseum.

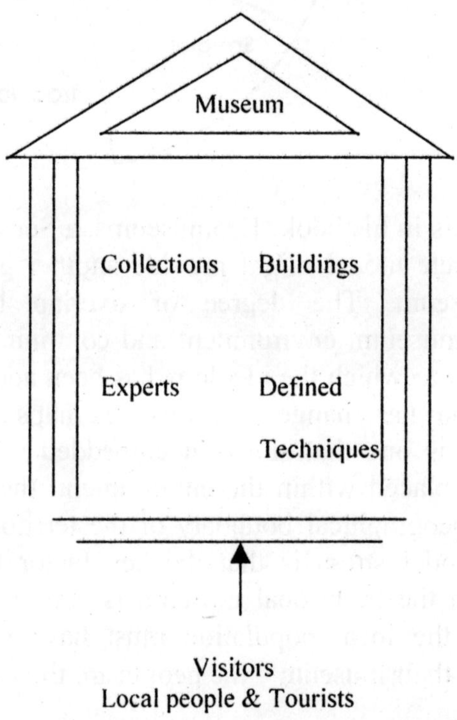

The traditional museum (after Rivard)

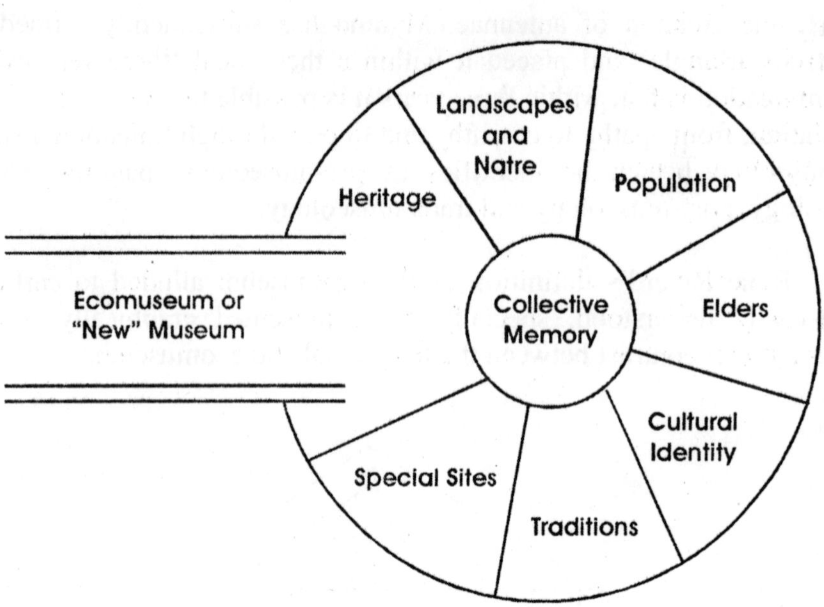

Peter Davis in his book 'Ecomuseums, a Sense of Place' suggested that the three circle model might provide another graphic representation for the ecomuseum. The degree of overlap between the circles representing ecomuseum, environment and community can give us some idea of the degree to which the ideology has been adopted and how far the traditional museum has changed. However, perhaps a better model for the true ecomuseum is one that shows it embedded within the community, which is in turn placed within the environment, the outer circumference then marks the geographical boundary of the territory. He believes what each of these model stress is that the key factor that differentiates an ecomuseum from the traditional museum is community involvement. In the ecomuseum the local population must have primary and ultimate responsibility for their museum – the people are the Curators.

The ecomuseum is now firmly established in France, making the country a 'virtual laboratory' for the study of contemporary questions of cultural heritage and museological change. The ecomuseum occupies an important place in relation not only to museum culture but also to rural life and economic development and the growth of the movement in that country. Other countries specially those with close links to France, rapidly adopted the philosophy of the ecomuseum. Canada and specially francophone Qubec was in the forfront. In Scandinavia the idea of the ecomuseum was adopted and has evolved to promote the interpretation and enjoyment of the cultural heritage of extensive geographical areas. Peter Davis conducted a survey worldwide in 1998 and found there were some 166 ecomuseums in 25 countries.

The Ecomuseum Parameters

Peter Davis describes a museum in the little village of Gavalochori, lying in the foothills of mountains that tumble gently down to Souda Bay on the northern shores of the Mediterraneian island of Crete. The Gavalochori is an ecomuseum by every criterion that the philosophy and theory of ecomuseology demands. It was initiated by the community, is maintained by the community, has a defined territory, links to other sites in the vicinity which have been preserved in situ, is part of a greater co operative venture and supports local development. However, it does not use the title 'ecomuseum' and the people who curate the collections and the built in structures are unaware of the concept. He again stated, there are some organizations that use the term 'ecomuseum' without any justification whatsoever. These include traditional museums of zoology, small museums devoted to environmental issues etc. which have adopted the term without real involvement with their local community or its development. There are again certain museums, which are using the term and have selectively adopted parts of the eco museum philosophy that suit their situation. Considering all these conditions, Peter Davis has questioned whether the term ecomuseum is just a myth or a figment of the museological imagination and if so whether there is any validity of the term.

As answer to all the above questions, Peter Davis had again suggested few indicators. He also took care of the Hamrin and Hulander's list of attributes of ecomuseum, which delineate that the ecomuseum :-

- covers a wide area

- consists of selected environments in the cultural landscape
- demonstrates what, where and how things took place in their original setting
- strives to explain what, where and how
- strives to preserve, restore and reconstruct
- strives to activate the visitor and make the cultural heritage accessible
- is founded on the interaction between culture and tourism
- cares for what already exists
- is based on the joint efforts of local authorities, associations, organizations, companies and private individuals
- is dependant on active voluntary efforts
- aims to make a little known district accessible to tourists
- appeals to local inhabitants is an effort to create a feeling of local identity
- appeals to schools and education at all levels
- is in a continuous process of evolution, where new features and improvements both long term and short term are introduced into the development programme
- aims to show the whole – from the general to the specific
- collaborates with artists, craftsmen, writers, actors and musicians

- promotes research by means of study circles and at an academic level

- aims to illustrate the connection between technology and the individual, between nature and culture, between past and present, between then and now.

The above attributes are worthwhile in examining and by doing so it is possible to analyse the diversity of ecomuseum activities, compare ecomuseums with traditional museums and explore the factors that might be identified as ecomuseum parameters.

Geographical Scale

Every museum, ecomuseum or not, has a territory, be it a national, regional or local. For the traditional museum it is the concept of geographical territory that helps the museum define its scope policies and a 'users' territory that frequently equates with political boundaries and the available resources. The ecomuseum concept of territory is different, in that it can more readily step beyond the artificial boundaries imposed by authority and select territories that are limited by topography, dialect, architecture, history, economy or customs. It is therefore the nature of the concept of territory that enables a distinction to be made between the ecomuseum and the traditional museum, not size. Ecomuseums can work at any scale that is considered most beneficial and most appropriate. An ecomuseum on a limited geographical scale, perhaps helping a small local community to establish its identity and promoting development, is just as valid an approach as one that covers hundreds of square kilometers and is geared to sustainable tourism.

Interpreting selected environments in the cultural landscape – in situ conservation

The idea of the in situ preservation and interpretation of sites does appear to hold true for most ecomuseums. It is real ecomuseum indicator. The majority of ecomuseums have a central administrative base and a number of dispersed sites that together attempt to portray a holistic view of their region.

Interpreting what, where and how – preserving, restoring, reconstructing

There is no substantive difference between the role of the ecomuseum and the traditional museum when considering the basic functions of interpretations and conservation. Both types of organization are attempting to preserve fragments of the heritage which may be a site, monument, an object, a rare breed or examples of local oral tradition and help people to understand its significance.

Interpreting what, where and how – preserving, restoring, reconstructing

There is no substantive difference between the role of the ecomuseum and the traditional museum. But interpretation should be site based, so demonstrating the significance of place and conservation or restoration should reflect a commitment from the local community to its heritage. All the activities should be supported by local community. Reconstruction again in terms of the fabrication of buildings or site-based features is however a common practice at site museums, a useful tool for interpretation.

Activating the visitor and making the cultural heritage accessible

Ecomuseum encourages the visitor to travel beyond the walls of the museum and experience a wide range of cultural and natural heritage sites. 'Activation' is perhaps also a reflection of the desire of the ecomuseum to create a link, arguably a spiritual and personal one, between the visitor and the environment, between the visitor and the region, to try and convey the elusive concept that is a 'sense of place'.

Ecomuseums are founded on the interaction between culture and tourism

This is a 'Scandinavian' ecomuseum point of view. It is quite deviated concept from the original ecomuseum concept, though communication with the visitors is always present.

Ecomuseums care for what already exists

This statement seems to stress the importance of the connection with the past, with the history of the people of the region and the tangible and intangible evidence has survived within the ecomuseum's territory. However this is a characteristics of most museums and is therefore not a distinguishing feature.

Ecomuseums are based on the joint efforts of local authorities, associations, organizations, companies and private individuals:

Ecomuseums are usually a cooperative venture. This is specially true when considering sources of financial support. However, it is also an indication that the ecomuseum plays an important role as a catalyst to joint initiatives.

Ecomuseums are dependent on active voluntary efforts

This statement is true for majority of ecomuseums whereas exceptions are also there. Most museums use volunteer for wide range of purposes like documentation, research, curatorial activities, visitor services etc.

Ecomuseums aim to make a little known district accessible to tourists

Ecomuseums have emerged in places that are trying to assert their cultural identity, that they are places with a low tourist profile. In such cases creation of a ecomuseum could be seen as one way to make a place better known to wider world.

The ecomuseum appeals to local inhabitants in an effort to create a feeling of local identity

The significance of local identity is central to the philosophy of the ecomuseum and is undoubtedly an important ecomuseum indicator. However it should be stressed that the ecomuseum does not simply appeal to local inhabitants, it is not simply a matter of purveying a view of local identity for consumption by local people but a process that should actively involve them in creating their own identity.

Ecomuseums appeals to schools and education at all levels

All ecomuseums communicate effectively and have dedicated educational programmes aimed at al age groups and to all levels of ability.

The ecomuseum is a continuous process of evolution where new features and improvements both long term and short term are introduced into the development programme

The ecomuseum is free to develop its activities in whatever ways are most beneficial to local community. Many ecomuseums fall beyond the boundaries of rigid local government control, which again suggests freedom of action and the adoption of novel ideas.

Ecomuseums aim to show the whole – from general to specific

A holistic approach to the interpretation of the cultural and natural heritage of a defined territory is central to the ecomuseum concept. The implication of such an approach is that as many different sites as possible should be interpreted and that interconnections between the sites and between culture and nature are fully explained.

Ecomuseums collaborate with artists, craftsmen, writers, actors and musicians

Many ecomuseums are devoted to rural crafts, agriculture, industrial processes and maritime history and document the intangible heritage (oral tradition, music, folklore) in addition to sites and objects. The interpretation of such resources, while achievable using traditional techniques (labels or guided tour), is made more meaningful and enjoyable by observing craftsmen, 'living history' events and listening to live music. Many of the ecomuseums make full use of such skills. However this is not an exclusive ecomuseum factor as many open air museums or historical sites also adopt this technique.

The ecomuseum promotes research by means of study circles and at an academic level

A number of ecomuseum bring together groups of local individuals and encourage them to research a particular aspect of their area. This is very much prevalent in the ecomuseums of Canada.

The ecomuseum aims to illustrate the connection between technology and the individual, between nature and culture, between past and present, between then and now

This statement expresses once again the holistic nature of the ecomuseum and its role in conserving the past for use in the present.

The evaluation of the significance of potential ecomuseum indicator is inconclusive, primarily due to the variety of ways in which the ecomuseum has evolved. The details of these parameters and their relevance in terms of the proposed site of north Guwahati, Assam has been discussed in later chapters. Ecomuseums frequently share characteristics with traditional museums and while some ecomuseums may exhibit a particular character others do not. Thus, some ecomuseums promote economic development via tourism and others do not; some may promote and publish research, most do not. Despite these grey areas, the following list of indicators can be applied to most ecomuseums:

- The adoption of a territory that is not necessarily defined by conventional boundaries.
- The adoption of a fragmented-site policy which is linked to in-situ conservation and interpretation.
- Conventional views of site ownership are abandoned; conservation and interpretation of sites via liaison and cooperation.

- The empowerment of local communities; the involvement of local people in museum activities and in the creation of their cultural identity.
- The potential for interdisciplinary and holistic interpretation.

Boylan (1992: 29-30) produced a similar list of characteristics that allows museums to measure how 'ecomuseological' they are. His five key concepts were

- Territory
- Fragmentation and the nature of ecomuseum 'collections'
- Interdisciplinary approaches to interpretation
- The nature of the ecomuseum 'customer'
- Local democracy and community empowerment.

He suggested that if each of these five characteristics is ranked on a scale from 1 (traditional approach) to 5 (ecomuseum approach), then a score of 13 or below indicates a traditional museum, 14-19 is an outgoing community centered museum with an interest in the environment and a score of 20+ identifies a true ecomuseum. He is of the opinion that tested against this scale many organizations that call themselves ecomuseums would fall within the center category (that is, they are not really ecomuseums). Peter Davis supported this ranking system. He said that this ranking might be considered a measurement of the amount of overlap between museum, environment and community. However he also suggests that anyone looking at ecomuseums with an unprejudiced eye could only conclude that they demonstrate a very significant amount of variation.

Peter Davis summarized the whole discussion on the concept of ecomuseum as follows:

- A pure form of the ecomuseum evolved in France, steeped in a new philosophy.

- The ecomuseum has evolved in many different ways and few museums that call themselves as ecomuseum now conform to the original models.
- Variations in the types of ecomuseum have appeared since greater emphasis has been placed on specific aspects of the original model.
- A new form of fragmented ecomuseum has evolved which has reacted to the economic needs of communities and the potential to capitalize on tourism (the 'Scandinavian ecomuseum model')
- Museums have been founded all over the world which are ecomuseums in everything but name.
- New museology was responsible for the rise of these new kinds of museums, which have adopted many names including 'community museum'
- The ecomuseum philosophy has gradually been adopted by more traditional institutions, museums have begun to step beyond the boundaries of buildings and identify themselves as apart of a wider heritage movement.
- As a result of the diversification of ecomuseums and the appropriation of ecomuseum characteristics by other more traditional establishments, it has become increasingly difficult to distinguish what an ecomuseum is and what it is not.
- The absence of a precise definition of an ecomuseum means that any organization can appropriate the title. Thus, any museum with an interest in the environment or community development can justify the title of ecomuseum if it wishes to adopt it.

If we consider Flaubert's observation, it comes to know that it is not the pearls that make a necklace but the thread provides a useful metaphor for the ecomuseum. If the ecomuseum is thought of as a thread, it can then be perceived as the mechanism that holds together the varied elements that make individual places special. If the 'Scandinavian ecomuseum model' is identified as one type of museum that can now justify the term, the thread of the ecomuseum will string together the various sites in its territory. Thus, if we think of the ecomuseum thread beyond the sites themselves, it comes up as the Rivard's model. Here, the pearls are the elements of landscape, nature, community, sites, song, traditions and so on. This necklace model helps us to understand that by combining the attributes of regions, their cultural sites and associated histories and themes, vernacular architecture, traditions, dialect, memories – the ecomuseum brings together those elements that make places special.

Prospects of Ecomuseums in India

Indian museum movement started in 1784 with the establishment of the Asiatic Society of Bengal, though the tradition of collection is age old practice in India. It is evident from the chitrasalas, cave and rock paintings and also the temples. The early 11th century temple of Brihadisvara at Tanjavur is the richest assemblage of sculpture and inscriptions. In fact the temples fully served not only as cultural center but also as educational and social centers besides a center for entertainment.

Regardless of above mentioned centers where rich collection were preserved in fact the museum movement started with the setting up of the Oriental Museum in Calcutta in 1814 by the Asiatic Society of Bengal. Its purpose was to house the miscellaneous objects of art, archaeology and natural history that were being accumulated by the exploratory activities of the society. The Oriental museum later developed into the Indian Museum, as it came to be so called in 1866. It was shifted to its present building in 1875 and thrown open to the public on 1st April 1878. Thus, the first museum of the country was born.

During British rule several other museums were set up. Remarkable among them, the Government Museum at Mathura (1874), Madras Govt. Museum, Victoria Technical Institute at Madras as a museum of crafts, Victoria Memorial Hall, Central Museum, Nagpur etc. The museum movement in India was boosted up by the establishment of Museums Associations of India in 1944, but true modern museum established after independence, was the National Museum of India. The museum was established on 15th August, 1949 in the Durbar Hall of Rashtrapati Bhawan, New Delhi. Subsequently, a new building suitable for the purpose was constructed and the collection which had grown since its inception was transferred to the new building where works of art were elegantly displayed on scientific lines and thrown open to the public on 18th Dec, 1960. Dr. Grace Morley was the first Director of the museum who started a new era of development of museums in India.

In 1970, ICOM started a chapter in India which helped to promote the cause of museums in India. The ICOM chapter provided Indian museums and museum personnel with a living link with the international museum world of the ICOM and enabled all concerned to make day to day consultations on their problems, attend professional meetings organized by the ICOM, contribute papers and communicate their achievements to the ICOM.

During the same period, a new practice and philosophy entered in the field of museum, called 'new museology', which is a post modernism theory. Though the concept of 'new museum' and 'ecomuseum' is not same, yet the basic concern of both the theory is community involvement, which is shared by other theories of museums like community museum, open air museum, neighbourhood museum etc. also. The ecomuseum movement started in France. With the international link through ICOM, eminent museum personnel of India like Dr. Sachin Roy, Dr. V.H. Bedekar etc. also contributed to the ecomuseum movement. A new tradition started in India, and it received full attention when a all India seminar on 'New Museology and Indian Museums' was organized in Bhopal during the All India Museums Association (MAI) Conference and accordingly a seminar was organized in Guwahati in the year 1988. The seminar was instrumental in the adoption and development of new Museology in India, considering the concepts, philosophy and practices of the exponents of the ecomuseology and new Museology in 1988. It included community participation, community initiatives, community ownership and conituous community support, desirability of identifying territory, concept of decentralization of works etc. which represent the major strength of this movement. Though this seminar was not entirely on ecomuseum yet, this is important here to discuss the declaration of this seminar as it has been considered as one of the most important development in the field of ecomuseum in India.

Historical Dimensions and Ecomuseum

The civilization of India is continuing for last more than 5000years. No country on earth has such a long cultural continuity, though there were more ancient civilizations notably in Egypt and Iraq. These were virtually overlaid by new intrusive cultures. On the other hand in India, the Brahman still repeats in his daily worship Vedic hymns composed over 4000 years ago and tradition recalls heroic chieftains and the great battles fought by them at about the same time.

The pre-Vedic Harappa culture bequeathed to later times sacred animals and trees, the Mother Goddess, the preoccupation with personal cleanliness and less certainly other aspects of Indian culture. From the Vedic Aryans came many of the Gods and Goddesses, the Vedic hymns, some of most important personal rituals of Hinduism, the patriarchal and patrilineal family system and the horse. Later Vedic times (1000-600BC) brought the passion for speculation on ultimate causes, the quest for the Absolute, the doctrine of transmigration, the search for release from the round of rebirth and mystical gnosis. In social life and material culture the same period saw the crystallization of the four classes (*varnas*) of Hindu society, the introduction of iron from western Asia, the domestication of the elephant, the development of kingdoms out of tribal chieftainships.

In the 300 following years coined money became common and writing known in the time of the Harappa culture and later forgotten became widespread. Heterodox teachers, chief of whom was the Buddha, spread new doctrines, which by passed the gods, the Vedas and the Brahmins and the area of civilization steadily expanded into the remote parts of the subcontinent.

Political developments over the preceding led to the first great empire of India that of the Mauryas, when for the first time most of the subcontinents were united under a single government. This period (c 320-185BC) produced the Machiavellian system of statecraft associated with the name of the minister Kautilya, the reputed author of the famous '*Arthasastra*'. From the Mauryas also come the earliest surviving stone sculpture of India, the oldest artificial caves and the most ancient Buddhist stupas. Under Asoka (c. 272-232BC) Buddhism increased its influence and was taken to Ceylon.

The 500years between the Mauryas and the Guptas (c.184BC-320AD) saw tremendous development in Indian civilization, partly due to fresh influences brought in by various invaders and traders and partly the result of internal developments. New forms of devotional religion emerged, centering round the gods Vishnu and Shiva and these led to the composition of the Bhagavad-Gita, now the most influential text of Hinduism. Buddhism developed a theology, the Mahayana, which was carried to China. Schools of law appeared, codifying in written form earlier traditions. The two great epics of India, the Mahabharata and the Ramayana were edited. Courtly literature began developing out of vanished prototypes: drama, ranging from the heroic to the sentimental and verse wonderful in its polish and ingenuity yet often filled with deep and sincere feeling. Logically reasoned philosophical schools emerged as distinct from the older religious teachers, most of whose arguments were analogical. Contact with South-East Asia became closer with the spread of trade and that region began to adopt many features of the religion and culture of India. These are only a few of the many innovations of this, perhaps the most formative period of Indian history before the 19th century.

The period from the rise of the Guptas to the death of Harshavardhana (320-647) can truly be called the classical period of Indian civilization. In this age the greatest sculpture of ancient India was produced and the finest literature written in the poems and plays of Kalidasa. This was the time of the best surviving ancient mural painting, typified by Ajanta. Knowledge grew also in this period. India's most important practical contribution to the world, the system of place notation of numerals, with nine digits and a zero, was known by 500AD and led to the great development of Indian mathematics and astronomy. The recording of ancient legends and traditions in the puranas began. The Mother Goddess, after centuries of neglect, became an important object of worship again. Stone-built temples appeared throughout the land.

Between the death of Harshavardhana and the coming of Islam (c.647- 1200 AD) the ecstatic devotional religion (*bhakti*) associated with the singing of hymns in the common tongue appeared in Tamilnadu, later to spread all over the subcontinent. Temples became larger and grander with spiring towers. The system of *hatha yoga* was developed and tantrism with its sacramentalization of sex spread in both Hinduism and Buddhism. In Sankara and Ramanuja Hindu religious philosophy saw its greatest teachers. Some of the finest schools of bronze casting in the world appeared in Bengal and Tamilnadu. The former region also developed a fine school of miniature painting.

With the coming of Islam fresh cultural influences made themselves felt. The Sultanate period (1192-1526 AD) saw the introduction of new styles of architecture, bringing the dome and arch. New schools of miniature painting, both Muslim and Hindu emerged. Sufi teachers disseminated the doctrines of Islam and helped to make the religious climate of northern India favourable to the spread of popular devotional Hinduism from the south. Paper was introduced, slowly replacing the traditional Indian writing materials – palm leaf and birch bark. The Urdu language began to appear as the lingua franca of northern India and poets began to compose in the everyday language instead of classical Sanskrit.

The great days of the Mughal Empire (1526-1707) witnessed the perfection of the schools of Muslim architecture and miniature painting, with the production of such splendid buildings as the Taj Mahal at Agra. Cannon and smaller fire arms began to be used in warfare. Europeans established trading stations at various ports and through them, specially the Portuguese new crops were introduced into India, among them the potato, tobacco, the pineapple and surprisingly, the spice which nowadays is commonly thought typical of India, the chilli pepper. The Sikh religion was born just as this period began, as a small devotional sect and at about the time when the period concluded it was reborn as a martial brotherhood to play an important part in the confused political life of he following century.

The 18th century saw the break up of the Mughal Empire and the steady expansion of the power of the British East India Company. It was a time of general cultural decline in India, but the genius of the land was still at work. The Urdu language little used hitherto as a medium of literary expression became the vehicle of great poetry at the decadent courts of Delhi and Lucknow; while in the Himalayan foothills, at the end of the century at the petty courts of local maharajas, by some unexplainable miracle, there worked painters who produced works of unprecedented beauty and sensitivity. With the 19th century the subcontinent was exposed to the full force of western influence and innovations are too numerous to list.

This cursory survey of the history of cultural change in India is sufficient in itself to show that as long as civilization has existed there, the country has never been stagnant, but has steadily developed through the ages. India has enjoyed over 4000years of civilization and every period of her history has left something to the present day.

As well as this great legacy of the human past, the people of the subcontinent have another inheritance from the nature itself – the land and its climate. In this sense perhaps India's most important inheritance is the great chain of the Himalayas, without which the land would be little more than a desert.

South of the Himalayas lie the great plains of the subcontinent, the centers from which civilization expanded in ancient times. Composed of deep silt carried down by the rivers Indus (Sind, Sindhu) and Ganga, these plains are naturally vey fertile but for centuries they have supported a dense population whose peasants used the most easily available form of manure, cow dung as fuel. In ancient days, however, the fertility and the healthy well-fed peasantry of India were noticed by foreign travelers from the Greek Megasthenes (c.300BC) onwards.

South of the Ganga are the Vindhya mountains and the long and beautiful river Narmada, dividing the north from the plateau region of

Maharashtra, generally called Deccan. The region less naturally fertile than the great plains has been for at least 2000years the home of tough martial peasants who, whenever energetic leadership appeared to consolidate their clans would take advantage of the political weakness of their neighbours to raid the wealthier lands to the north, south east and south. The Deccan plateau becomes steadily less rugged and more fertile as one proceeds south and south east. Along the eastern littoral of the peninsula are fertile riverine plains, the most important historically being that of Tamilnadu, reaching from Madras to Kanyakumari. Here, over 2000years ago, the Tamil people developed a fairly advanced civilization independently of the Aryan north, this region has throughout history maintained a consciousness of its differences from the north and has cherised its own language, while remaining part of the whole Indian cultural area, there may be an analogy between the Tamil attitude to the northern Aryans and that of the Welsh to the English, with the difference that while many Welshmen have English as their mother tongue, few if any Tamils have a mother tongue other than Tamil.

Yet another inheritance of India from the distant past is her people. Despite the difficult mountain passes and the wide seas baring access to India, people have been finding their way there from the days of the Old Stone Age, when small hordes of primitive men drifted into the subcontinent. These are probably the ancestors of one of India's three main racial types-the proto-australoid, so called because of the resemblence to the Austarlian aborigines. In India the most pure Proto-Australoid type is to be found among the tribal peoples of the eilder parts of the peninsula, but proto Australoid features can be traced almost everywhere in the subcontinent, specially among people of low caste. The ideal type is short, dark skinned, broad nosed and large mouthed.

The next main stratum in the population of India is the Palaeo-Mediterranean often loosely called Dravidian. These people seem to have come to south Asia from the west, not very long before the dawn of civilization in the Indus valley and they may have contributed to the foundation of the Harappa culture. Graceful and slender with well chiseled features and aquiline noses, the ideal type is particularly to be found among the better class speakers of Dravidian languages but it also occurs everywhere in the subcontinent.

Then in the 2nd millennium BC, came the Aryans, speakers of an indo European language which was the cousin of hose of classical Europe. Some have suggested that these people came in two or more waves, the earlier invaders being round headed (brachycephalic) people of the type called alpine or armenoid and the later long headed folk, typical caucasoids, similar in build to northern Europeans. Long before they entered India the people who called themselves Aryans had intermixed with other peoples and their advent meant a severe cultural decline, which lasted for many centuries. Only when Aryan culture was fertilized by the indigenous culture did it begin to advance, to form the classical civilization of India.

These three, the proto-australoid, the palaeo-mediterranean and the Caucasoid or indo European are the most strongly represented racial types among the inhabitants of India, but they are by no means the only ones. Almost every race of central Asia found its way to India. Turks provided the ruling families in much of what is now Pakistan long before the coming of the Muslims, who were also Turks. Mongolians of various races have been entering India over the Himalayan and north eastern passes since long before history. The Muslim ruling classes imported numerous African slaves who have long since merged with the general population, Persian and Arab traders settled along the west coast from before the Christian era. Some married Indian women and the descendants have become indistinguishable from the rest of the population. Others, such as the small but vigorous Parsi community have kept their stock pure. The various European traders and conquerors have left their mark also. Along the west coast of India and Ceylon an appreciable quantity of Portuguese blood circulates in the veins of the general population, while elsewhere in India the so called Anglo-Indian community is the result of many marriages and liaisons between European soldiers and traders and Indian women.

Thus, a brief of the history of Indian civilization discussed above. This is a fact that India's enduring inheritance of climate, land and people, the basis on which its high civilization has been built and which will remain more or less unchanging to condition the lives of its people in all their triumph and vicissitudes in future centuries.

The manifestation of this civilization can be catagorised as ecomuseums. There can be network of these different categories of ecomuseums complementing each other in conservation and preservation of this age old products of civilization. Because of this interface there exists the structural survivors – the approach widely accepted in Social Anthropology. Following are some of the probable categories of ecomuseums in India:

Following are some of the probable categories of ecomuseums in India:

- Sacred complexes of India, for example, Kashi, Gaya, Mathura, Vrindaban, Brihadeswar etc. These holy places of India form a sacred *kshetra* with their sacred geography, sacred specialists and sacred performances and the whole *kshetra* can be converted into ecomuseums.
- Significant ethnic groups of India. The list is so vast with so many racial groups (as discussed above), with their unique identity can form one kind of ecomuseums. For example, the Naga youth dormitory – which is a unique institution for social and cultural education and development among the youths. This could be another category.
- World heritage sites of India like the Majuli-great river island of the world in Assam, Darjeeling Himalayan Railway, Bhimbedka Rock Art sites etc, can be some other unique ecomuseums.
- Rajasthan – the abode of kings and Princes posses several unique *havelis* (palaces). The nobles of the Royal Court were given some *thikanas* (circles) such as Alwar which had huge *havelis* as well as forts. They can be converted to ecomuseums. The inhabitants of each *thikana* will be the local community. These *thikanas* are now loosing their year old charm due to negligence of their owner. So, converting them to ecomuseum will be another effort to preserve the heritage.

- In the Royal Court of Princely States of Rajasthan, there prevalent the system of 36 karkhanas (departments). Each of the department were engaged in different activities. These departments can be converted into ecomuseum. With each of these departments a community was involved who were experts in that particular skill. They even belong to one particular caste also. So, converting these departments within a particular territory where the community involved reside, a very unique ecomuseums can emerge. For example, the artists of Suratkhana were given a particular area to reside and prepare paintings. The descendants of these artists are still there and they still practice their traditional occupation. Though they have gone through modern education, yet each member of an artists family knows the technique of paintings of Jaipur School. Again, there was a caste locally called '*Khati*'. They are carpenters and there was a department called '*khatikhana*'. They still practice their traditional occupation.
- Korlai in the coastal plains of the Arabian sea in the west reveal an imprint of cross cultural interface. Here western and eastern heritages preserved by the communities reveals local identity. Such an ideal situation could be explored for the ecomuseum set up.

References

Anon, 'The Ecomuseum', *Newsletter of the ICOM Natural History Committee*, 1978

Bedekar, V.H., *New Museology for India*, New Delhi, 1995

Boylan, P., 'Ecomuseums and the new museology – some definitions', *Museum Journal* 92(4), 1992

Corsane, G. and Holleman, W. 'Ecomuseums: a brief evaluation', *Museums and the Environment*, South African Museums Association, Pretoria, 1993

Davis, P., *Ecomuseums A Sense of Place*, London and New York, 1999

Rivard, R., 'Museums and ecomuseums-questions and answers', *Okomuseumsboka – identiet, okologi, deltakelse*, Norway, 1988

Viet, J. (ed.), *The International Thesaurus of Cultural Development*, UNESCO, Paris, 1980.

Chapter 4

Ecomuseums Worldwide

Ekomuseum Berslagen

Location : Central Sweden

Area : 750 sq k.m.

Community : The residents of the mining and industrial region who share common industrial and social history.

Aim : It aims to conserve and interpret the physical remains of the 2,000 years industrial tradition of the area and also the social history it represents.

Significant Features : This museum was opened with a mission to provide support for local people and to attract tourists. Smedjebacken, Ludvika and Angelsberg became key centre's and it has a network of some 50 cultural sites. The sites include various mines and miners villages, furnaces and forges, Finnish villages, a museum and the world's oldest surviving oil refineries. This Ecomuseum involves the entire local community for all its activities thus keeping the community spirit alive.

Remarks : This Ecomuseum is established to preserve the industrial heritage of the territory along with the social and cultural heritage associated with it. The community was involved to raise awareness of their industrial tradition and social history.

Ecomusee Pays de Rennes

Location : Rennes is in South West of Paris, France.

Area : The whole area of Rennes Ecomuseum comprises of La Bintinais farm and about 20 hectares of meadows, orchards, livestock and pond with a picnic area.

Community : The local residents of Rennes area.

Aim : To tell a real story with the utmost scientific rigour and connect past and present. To preserve and exploit a cultural heritage tied to a rural society in the process of extinction due to massive and rapid urbanization of Rennes through solid scientific base given by experts, scholars and academics.

Significant Features : The La Bintinais farm and surrounding site comprises the Ecomuseum. The exhibition surface inside the Bintinais farm, perfectly restored recreates the farmhouse interior of the late 19th century. The most fascinating activities of the Ecomuseum are those related to the preservation of domesticated plants and animals. Temporary exhibitions and special activities take place throughout the year. (ploughing with horses, honey production, grafting fruit trees, pig fairs, apple fairs) provide additional attractions and contribute to in situ interpretation of the site.

Remarks : This Ecomuseum is established to preserve the rural agricultural heritage. This museum has a living collection of rare breed of domestic animals and about 60 varieties of cider, apples and other crop plants.

Ecomuseu Municipal do Seixal

Location : Portugal. Municipal region of Seixal is a short ferry ride from the capital Lisbon.

Area : It is a multinucleus museum with seven principal sites.

Community : Local people of Seixal municipality.

Aim : To protect and conserve the cultural and natural heritage, disseminate traditional local knowledge in the municipality of Seixal, placing the onus on in situ conservation according to the principal of the functional rehabilitation of museological assets and divulgement of the museums work among the local community.

Significant Features : The original base of the museum, the Quinta de Palace, now acts as one of the principal stores for reserve collections. In May 1982 the Ecomuseum moved its headquarters to a school at Torre de Marinha. This site works as the documentation, education and information centre devoted to the history of seixal and its people. These two sites are among the six that comprise the Ecomuseum.

The other sites include a renovated shipyard at Arrentela , a Roman archaeological site at Quinta do Rouxinal and a tide mill. There are 12 well preserved watermills in the Seixal region. The watermill site enables the visitor to see the milling equipment in action and millers cottage. A waterwheel has been adopted as the logo of the Ecomuseum, a symbol of revived and reviving energy.

Remarks : This museum is spread across seven principle sites thus making it multi nucleus. This museum works with the participation and involvement of local people from every walk of life for e.g. factory workers explained the operation of machinery in the museum, local sailors helped visitors to learn sailing and navigation skills and so on. In many respects this museum has many features of conventional local museum e.g. it has significant archives and documentation facilities, and considerable collections of archaeology, ethnography, science and technology and maritime history. However an *in-situ* preservation policy, the fragmented nature of the museum and community participation justifies this museum to be called Ecomuseum.

Lake Toya Area Eco Museum

Location : Japan

Area : The Ecomuseum in the Lake Toya area is coordinated by 6 municipalities. To encourage this extensive area to implement the project, a common theme was established.

Community : Residents of the lake Toya region

Aim : A museum of nature in which visitors can discover the ''burning mountain" and history of "northern land" - By learning of the volcanic benefits, recognizing the earth endowed with nature and discovering the ways of living of ancestors. It aims in

a. Creation of opportunities for comprehensive study area for local people: By fostering the Ecomuseum in cooperation with local residents, they can deepend the understanding of local history, nature and culture to enhance their interests in the region
b. Passing down the history of the coexistence with the volcano - expectation of reduced future disasters – the past volcanic remains provide the history of the area which has coexisted with Mt. Usu. The preservation of the volcanic remains leads to preparation for educational opportunities for hazard prevention. By means of education programs for hazard prevention, the damage from future volcanic disasters can be reduced.
c. Promotion of regional development by resident participation - The Ecomuseum in the Lake Toya area is planned to be coordinated

and managed by 6 west-Iburi local public entities. This coordinating operation can encourage the travel of tourists among the areas and the interaction of local residents.

d. Promotion of new coordinating activities among neighboring areas - The Ecomuseum has a unique concept of "coexistence of areas proximate to the volcano", showing distinct features from other tourist spots.

e. Fostering of local industries and tourism- by developing various options such as guided tours, creating experience and outdoor activities, Ecomuseum can be expected to promote tourism and create new types of local industries

Significant Features : The eruption of Mt. Usu in March 2000 caused great damage in the lake Toya area. For early recovery from this disaster, an ecomuseum concept for this area was developed. The Lake Toya area also incurred a tremendous economic loss from the 2000 eruption of Mt. Usu such as a declining number of tourists to the area. By developing an Ecomuseum comprising natural resources and volcanic remains aimed at forming the Lake Toya area into a more attractive tourist spot and relaxing countryside. Currently, the remains of damage caused by the 2000 eruption have become a tourist attraction.

Based on local characteristics in the wide region of the Ecomuseum, three areas are defined. Each area is dedicated to conducting community development using their individual attractive features, and creating systematic coordination with other areas.

The ecomuseum's main theme and three areas are:

a. "Volcanic Boon (Remains)" Area

In the range within about 3 kilometers from the peak of Mt. Usu, there are many facilities and places where volcanic activity can be experienced and studied. More specifically, by visiting the still fuming Mt. Nishi, Mt. Kompira and Mt. Showa Shin-zan, people can learn the history of eruption in the Mt. Usu area. In addition, the sites of a collapsed hospital and west-

Iburi main fire station give visitors .the details on the damage by the eruption and activities for restoration.

b. *"Boon of the Earth and Culture" Area*

Lake Toya, Osaru River area. Experiencing *"bountiful nature"* feeling and appreciating the benefits of the countryside.

c. *"History of Ancestors and Marine Treasures" Area*

Coast of the Volcanic Bay following the"footsteps" of ancestors .Area for learning ancient wisdom, appreciating the benefits of the Volcanic Bay and understanding the lessons of the history.

Characterized by its marine benefits and its temperate region, this area gives opportunities to appreciate various historical values by visiting ancient remains and old buildings of the Date Clan, particularly Irie Kaizuka (cone shell-mounds) and Kita-kogane kaizuka. These shell-mounds are preserved by lively civil activities and visitors can expect to attend lectures filled with the atmosphere of the indigenous society.

Remarks : This Ecomuseum has a unique structure. It has one core centre and it is connected by 3 theme centers. This system was adopted to manage an extensive area in a proper manner. These two centers together play important roles in providing information and administering the organization of the museum. Core center and theme centers are further attached with satellites such as scenic spots, an observation deck, a resource center. Moreover walking trails connecting the satellites and network access roads contributes this ecomuseum.

Ha Long Bay Ecomuseum

Location : Vietnam

Area : Local community of Ha long area and neighbouring areas like Quangninh.

Aim : To bring together the World Heritage Area and the neighbouring communities of Quangninh to enhance resources for job creation, community cultural development, environmental education, sustainable tourism development and responsible local cultural heritage growth.

Significant features :

- The Ha long Eco-museum contains a variety of exhibits and displays about the entire region of the World Heritage Area and its hinterland. It provides a detail understanding of the Bay and its natural and cultural environment.
- It assists visitors to understand the various features of the Bay and provides them with a number of walks and tours, guided and self-guided, to explore the rich diversity of the local heritage. Visitors are able to enjoy quality and take home authentic experiences through the natural landscape, beautiful caves and interpretive tools, as well as from the entertainment and services available, such as: boats, speed boats, hydroplanes, balloons and cable cars.
- The Eco-museum Hub also provides facilities for study and research into the remarkable natural and cultural environment of the Bay, its conservation and management.

Remarks : The whole of the World heritage site and its hinterland are considered as an open Eco-museum. Therefore, Ha Long Bay Eco-museum is seen as a way of addressing culture in development through bringing people and their environment together.

The Danish Lake Museum (Ecomuseum Sohojlanders Okomuseum)

Location : Denmark

Aim : To strengthen and improve the presentation of the regions culture and nature in order to provide the locals and the many guests to the area with the best possible experiences and possibilities.

Area : Approx.1,719 square kilometers.

Structure : The ecomuseum is a co-operative venture between four museums and a nature centre. The Skandeborg Museum, located in an 18th C Ballif's house in the town is a focus for local history, while the Om Kloster Museum interprets monastic life and medicine in the middle ages at the ruins of a 12th C Cistercian monastery. The Ry windmill, built in 1872 became a museum in 1988 and also houses a museum of clog - making, which was a traditional industry in the region. The fresh water museum near Ry harbour is devoted to the ecology of lakes and rivers. Water power was very important in this region of Denmark and the Klostermolle Naturcenter is based in a former watermill and paper and pulp- making factory that was brought by the Ministry of Environment in 1975. Financial support for joint marketing of these sites, and their co-operative initiatives, is provided by the country council, three district councils and lottery funding, via the Council for the Country side.

Significant features : The vision statement for the ecomuseum is 'the development of themes....based on the human use of natural resources in the Central Jutland Lake District' and the considerable emphasis is placed on the need to interpret the landscape by 'making things alive'. Site preservation and interpretation are important projects for this ecomuseum, which identifies local people as the primary target group, 'as through the work of the ecomuseum they can obtain a better understanding of local identity and history.'

Remarks : Danish lake Ecomuseum is a an outcome of the sincere attempt made by the Government to provide the locals as well as the guest with first hand information, best possible experience and possibilities of the regions culture, art, tradition history and nature.

Ecomuseum in Guizhou

Community : Miaos, Dongs, Hans.

Significant Features : The rocky mountains of Guizhou, a province in south west China are an abode for different Chinese communities namely the Miaos, the Dongs, the Hans. They are small communities with distinct ethnic culture and tradition. Hence a sino-norwegian project began talking shape and developed ecomuseum in Guizou, where community in itself considered to preserve something, making everyone responsible to take care of the culture their cultural heritage, since it is urgent to do something at this stage of social developments, where the community people are leaving their indigenous culture and adapting modern traits and the outcome of this would be uncalled death of the cultural heritage of the minority community of China, due to the merging of villages into the mainstream culture.

Remarks : Initiative taken by the Sino-Norway government to protect the indigenous culture of ethnic minority territories in China marked the beginning of ecomuseum culture in China. Proper guidance by the scientific research corps of the Guangxi museum and zeal of the locals, made it possible for the locals to achieve their own cultural self awareness and scientific understanding. Development of "structural halls" and "display areas" have strengthened the villager's ability to interact with the outside world.

Staffin Ecomuseum –Ceumannan

Community : Staffins

Location : Scotland

Aim : To preserve and introduce the rich and fascinating history, nature, agricultural practices, religious, healing power of the indigenous plants, geological, archeological facts, traditional techniques of fishing etc of the staffins.

Significant Features : Staffin Ecomuseum has 13 original sites, each site is enstored with fascinating and exciting facts and information. The first site that is the township of Flodigarry narrates the history of staffins. Each site offers different experience altogether, be it traditional or geological facts of the extinct Dinosaurs's foot.

Remarks : Ecomuseum aims at community participation and also focuses on tourist inflow and many other ways to sustain the ecomuseum financially, however this very museum of Staffin is bit too commercialized and utilized more as a tourist destination.

Liehtalanniemi Ecomuseum., Puumala

Location **:** Finland, situated in the south savo countryside, the site of a small farm.

Area : The first in Finland. It encompasses some 23 hectares of open countryside, the site of a small farm. In 1851 the site consisted primarily of rock, forest, marsh and a small water meadow; there were neither buildings nor fields.

Aim **:** The original idea was the creation of a 'working Ecomuseum' inhabited by a family utilizing the surrounding natural resources, using the same methods and having a similar environment impact.

For practical reasons this proved impossible and other methods have had to be employed to create an 'authentic setting'. However, the guide brings life to the farm, aided by a team of volunteers who demonstrate traditional craft skills.

Structure : In 1851 the site consisted primarily of rock, forest, marsh and a small water meadow; there were neither buildings nor fields. Reclamation for agriculture gradually took place around the turn of the century, but the land was farmed in a traditional manner until the last owner died in 1978, when the farm was taken over by the state. It was then donated to the municipality of Puumala, which is responsible for its maintenance. The restoration and upkeep of the farm, and the cultivation of the land using traditional techniques (so preserving important wildlife habitats), is assisted by funding from the Worldwide Fund for Nature.

The poor quality of land meant that the owners of the smallholding had to be very resourceful, finding raw materials for fuel, buildings, and tools from the immediate surroundings and relying on the bounty of field, forest and lake for food. Fish were important additions to the diet and a variety of home-made nets and fish traps were constructed to catch them. Additional revenue was obtained by hunting foxes for their furs and seals to obtain oils that were used for medicinal purposes and for oiling leather. Today, Liehtala is preserved in a manner that recaptures the self-sufficient life style of a small holder- fisher family at the beginning of 20th C and the buildings, equipment, fields, meadows, woodlands, crops and livestock reflect this.

Ecomusee regional du centre, La Louviere

Location : Belgium, the province of Hainaut and the town of La louviere.

Aim : The industrial heart of the Centre area of Belgium was based around coalmining and associated heavy industries, including steel manufacture. The immigrants from many countries worked there. It is the interleaved story of immigration and industry that is interpreted by the Ecomuseum at its major site, a story that captures the essence of the area's identity and promotes pride in its past achievements. Centre is also an area rich in folklore, its rich racial mix bringing its own artistic, musical and literary traditions and distinctive material culture, features that are woven into the ecomuseum's exhibitions and activities.

Structure : Le Centre Miner is based around a coal mine that closed in 1973; the buildings on the site date from 1830. In addition to its winding's engines, pit-head tower and engineer's workshop, it also has reconstructed miner's cottages, blacksmiths and clog-makers shops and a permanent exhibition that retraces four centuries of coalmining in the region. It acts as a permanent documentation and administrative centre for the ecomuseum, housing documents and archives relating to coal mining, serves as a conference centre, stages temporary exhibitions, incorporates a cafeteria and bookshop and is the base for Ecomuseum education service.

The Ecomuseum Regional du Centre has three additional sites. At Strepy- Bracquegnies the white painted farmhouse of La Ferme Delsamee is dedicated to farming history, the permanent exhibition examining the evolution of harvesting techniques. All that remains of the monastery and farm of La Grande Louviere is its chapel built in 1533; now deconsecrated, it is used by the Ecomuseum to recount the ways of life under the Ancient regime. The old railway station at Haine-St Pierre, built in 1855 and closed in 1982, is used as an interpretive centre dedicated to steel workers and steel working. The ecomuseum has also produced a series of trail guides that enable the visitor to discover the region and its industrial past for themselves.

Run by a separate association, the ecomuseum works closely with the Cultural Affairs Department of the province of the Hainaut, which provides the majority of the budget; Eight permanent staff-historians, conservators, technicians and demonstrators- run the four sites, supported by the local volunteers.

Chapter 5

Prospects of an Eco Museum Site

A Perspective site of Assam

To experiment the paradigm and prospects of an ecomuseum site, a sacred complex of North Guwahati, Assam has been selected. Doul Govinda, the late medieval temple of Lord Krishna is situated at village Rajaduar of North Guwahati of Assam on the north bank of the river Brahmaputra, is a sacred complex, which is pivotal for the preservation of the Assamese culture in its totality.

This temple and its three surrounding traditional villages - Rajaduar, Madhyamkhanda and Shilsako shall be the designated territory for the study within the scope of ecomuseum as postulated by western Museologists. The entire landscape, both human and natural appears to be a potential territory for establishing an exclusive local identity of north Guwahati within a multicultural city of Guwahati.

The significance of the particular territory lies in the fact that, Rajaduar was the gateway for king. That implies its historical connection. The fact was confirmed from the copper plate found here of the king Dharampala, one of the ruler of Pala dynasty and the plate indicates that there was a palace earlier. (Das, 1968: 3-5) This particular territory is unique because of its historical, archaeological, ethnological, religious and artistic elements. Besides, typical hilly ecology with perennial undergrowth, a place having its own rural identity, within the urban set up of the city of Guwahati.

The significance of the defined territory in this case is based on a sacred complex with all its basic elements. The Doul Govinda temple has been the epitome of multiple human creativities in terms of tangible and intangible heritage, which is continuing for a long time. It has been attempted to show cultural dictionary of the Guwahati as the territory. The South Guwahati reveals a multicultural interface with strong urban traits whereas north Guwahati shows a unicultural identity with somewhat rural tinge.

Natural Heritage

Territorial identity

Doul Govinda temple complex and its three neighbourhood – Rajaduar, Shilsako and Madhyamkhanda of north Guwahati reveals a strong local identity so far as the socio-cultural, religious, historical aspects are concerned. The entire north Guwahati has been divided into four Wards and the Shilsako and Madhyamkhanda is in the block 3 and the Rajaduar is in block 4. In each village there are approximately 11000 villagers, according to 2000-2001 census.

Ecologically it has its emergence due to the interface of a river ecology and a hilly undulating terrain with evergreen undergrowth with rare species of plants and animals.

Topography

North Guwahati with its geographical and ecological diversity is a place of magical beauty. Its surrounding verdant forests, exquisite flora, turbulent streams, lofty mountains and majestic snow clad peaks make it a unique place. Nature has ungrudgingly blessed Assam with an abundance of scenic grandure, a wealth of rarest & near-extinct wildlife which has made it a parts of global bio-diversity 'hotspot'. North Guwahati shares this hotspot including including Golden Langur, Hoolock Gibbon, Pygmy Hog, Hispid Hare, White-Winged Wood duck, Tiger , Clouded leopard, Swamp Deer, Genetic Dolphins etc. Moreover, during season flock of resident & migratory birds make this place their natural habitat.

Kamrup District of Assam is one of the major districts of Assam with its capital being Guwahati. Though the boundary of earlier Kamrup is no more, yet this is the same Kamrup where Narakashur, Bhagadatta or Badan Barphukan ruled. The city of Guwahati has been divided into north and south by the river Brahmaputra. South Guwahati has now become the city of heterogeneous population, but north Guwahati is still remains intact.

Gateway to the seven states of North-east India and nestled in the Brahmaputra valley, Guwahati is surrounded by lush forests and green expanses of paddy fields. Awash with centuries-old temples, the city is the base to visit the wildlife sanctuaries. Guwahati houses the administrative capital of the state of Assam, Dispur, India. Apart from being a destination itself, it is the pivotal point for the tourists exploring the northeastern region of India. In addition to being a place of pilgrimage, Guwahati is the cultural hub and educational nerve center of North Eastern India. The unique feature to the ecology of Guwahati is its close proximity to Bhutan, eastern Himalaya, which reflects similar climatic condition and also the flora and fauna. The river ecology of Brahmaputra river is another specialty. The Brahmaputra river within Assam is 700km long. Guwahati is just on the bank of the river. There are legends regarding the river, which says it as the son of Lord Brahma. The sandy shores of the Brahmaputra often create temporary wetlands in winter, which provide shelter to Ferruginous Ducks and other water birds. Ferruginous Ducks

Map of Assam
Not to Scale

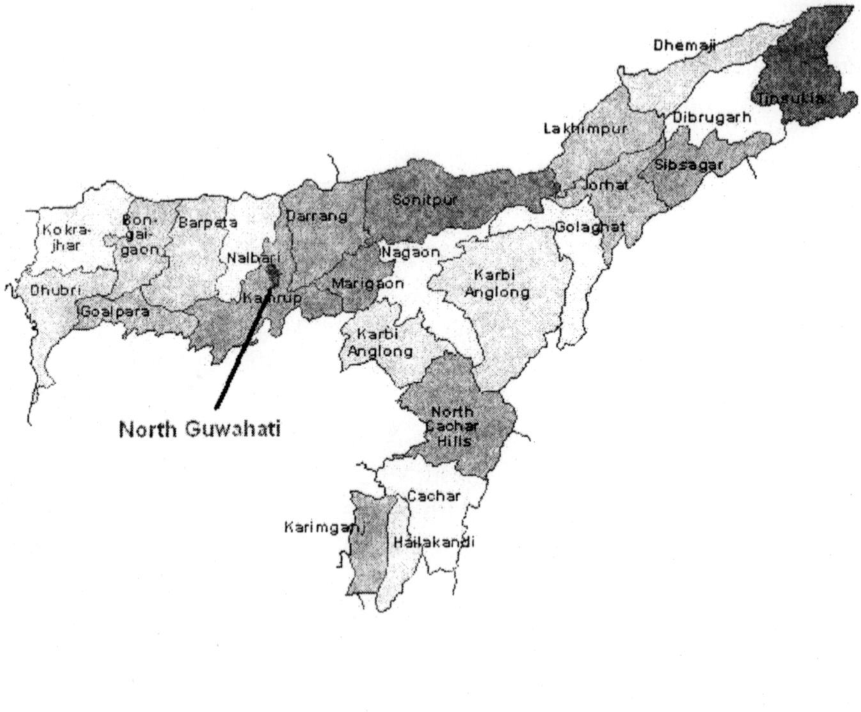

Map of North Guwahati

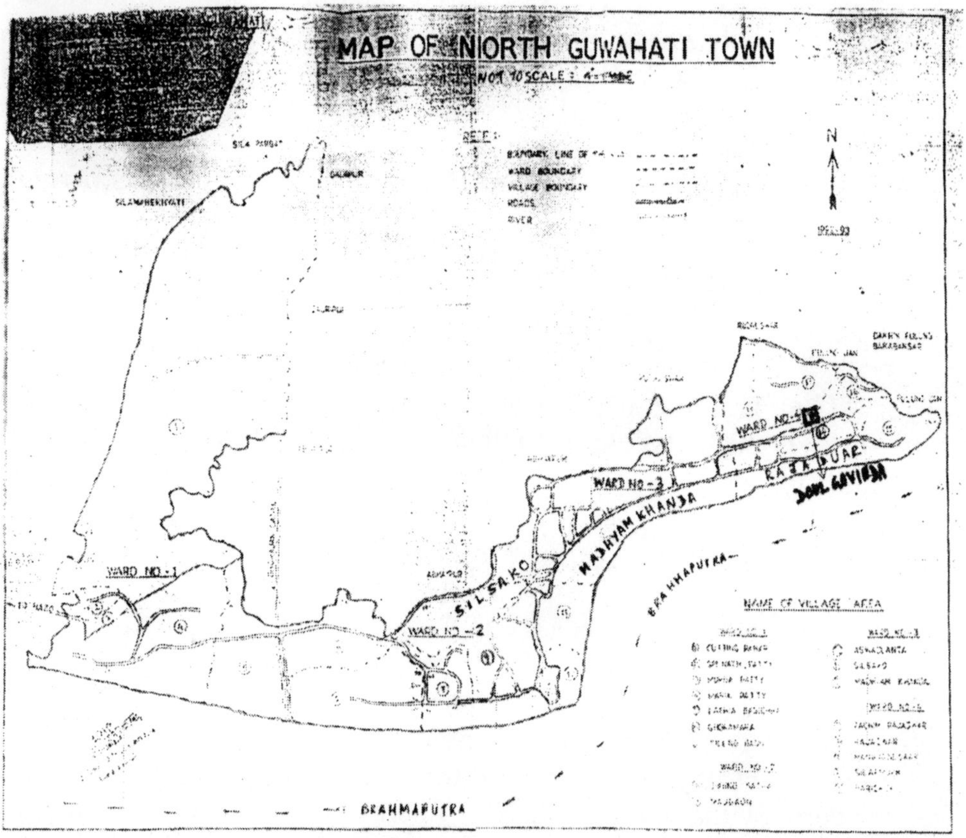
MAP OF NORTH GUWAHATI TOWN
NOT TO SCALE
WARD NO - 1
WARD NO - 2
WARD NO - 3
SILSAKO
MADHYAM KHANDA
RAJADUAR
DOUL GOVINDA
BRAHMAPUTRA
NAME OF VILLAGE AREA

have also been found on the main Brahmaputra river tract. The Brahmaputra river is an important flyway for many wintering birds.

North Guwahati is being regarded as the Kashi of the east. People believe that whoever dies in north Guwahati, gets the sacred death. It is in the midst of '*pancha tirtha*' (five places of pilgrimage) (Barua, 1985). One can have the holy views of *Manikarneswar*, *Dirgheswari*, *Ashwaklanta*, *Umananda*, the famous *kamakhya* by taking one stand by the Brahmaputra. This is the rare beauty of north Guwahati.

There are three branches of '*Satras*' and many temples here. In 16th century under the leadership of Sankarveda and his most favourite disciple Madhavadeva started wonderful movement of Neo-vaishnavism in Assam and 'Satras' are vaishnava monastry. Satras are like religious headquarters of vaishnavites. There are 715 Satras in Assam today.

There are three units of Satras here in north Guwahati which are also held in high esteem by religious people following the faith of vaishnavism, of all these Auniati satra branch attracts outsiders. The Garhmur Satra at Madhyam Khanda and Dihing Satra in Mazgaon area are also spreading the cult of Vaishnavism among the people

The Doul Govinda temple and its surrounding three neighbourhoods – Rajaduar, Shilsako and Madhyamkhanda is situated on the easternmost part of the historical town of North Guwahati, which had always been a sect of heroic and glorious achievements. It is a small town of panoramic beauty, on the bank of the river Brahmaputra. It is bounded on the north by the village Abhoipur, Rudreswar, Rangmahal; on the east by the Brahmaputra and its tributary Barnadi; on the south by the Brahmaputra and on the west by Amingaon, NF Railway line and Silamahkhaity. Amingaon is just on the bank of Brahmaputra. Recently an Export Promotion Industrial Park (EPIP) has been developed here. It is small industrial town adjacent to Guwahati city. Generally when we talk of north Guwahati we can not isolate the adjoining areas such as Gauripur, Rudreswar, Rangmahal on the north and *Sila* grant, Numaligarh on the west. The whole region covers an area of 8 sq. km.

Climate

The climate of north Guwahati is sub temperate. In other words, the climate is neither too hot nor freezing cold. The winter starts from the middle of October and continues till the middle of March. Thereafter the mercury continues rising till the onset of monsoons which start from the last week of May or early June and continues till the September.

However these figures may not be very stable every year as the monsoon and the great damage caused by the flood of river Brahmaputra the agriculture cycle gets highly affected.

Flora and fauna

The area is well stocked with rare birds and animals. To see the birds one does not have to go to the hills or the forests and search them. *Kuruwa* (Ring tailed Fishing Eagle (*Haliaeetus leucorythus*)-, *Rajdhanesh* (Great Pied Hornbill) (*Buceros bicornis homrai*)-, *Hetuluka (*Bluthroated Barbet (*Megalaima asiatica*), *Deo Hauh (*White Winged Wood Duck), *Himalayan woodpecker*, *Cuckoos* and *koels*, *orioles* and *magpies*, *swallows* and *shrikes*, *bee-eaters* and blue *jays*, *sun* birds and *munias*, *ioras* and *nuthatches*, *lapwings* and *wagtails*, *storks* and *egrets*, *moorhens* and *water cocks*, *ducks* and *cormorants* – all varieties of birds move about almost freely throughout the year close to human habitation. As mentioned earlier, the Brahmaputra river has given shelter to Ferruginous Ducks and other water birds. Besides, verdant forests and green expanses of paddy fields along with the wetland created by Brahmaputra has made possible for rare birds to migrate here from far away and also to nestled here. Naturalists have listed about 200 species of birds including many types of water birds and ducks in all over Assam.

Equally attractive is the rare animals of the area. There are so many species that are either exclusive to the area or rarely seen in any other part of the country.

The hollock gibbon – India's only ape, the stump tailored macaque, the capped langur and the golden langur monkeys are peculiar to Assam. The pigmy hog is found nowhere else in the world. The clouded leopard, the golden cat, the peculiar giant civet, the binturong, the hog badgers, porcupines, civet cats, gangetic dolphins, mongooses, giant squirrels and pythons are also frequently seen here.

Assam is blessed with unusually rich flora. Some of them indigenoius and others exotic` grow almost everywhere. Besides *Sal, Teak* and other valuable timber trees, which Assam grows in plenty, Assam's forests have the fullest range of tropical vegetation types – dry evergreen and wet evergreen.

The unique flora of the territory also includes bamboo and cane. Bamboo and cane is produced in large number in this area. The significance of these two are many. They play pivotal role in the socio economic and religious activities. The cane and bamboo products of Assam is famous world wide. Banana trees are also available equally. People use different parts of the plant for different purposes, specially, the bananas are offered as *prasad* in religious purpose, again *prasads* are offered in banana leaves only. The stem is used for offerings and again of few banana stems are used as one of the vegetable also. Likewise, bamboo shoot is one of the typical food items of Assamese people.

Human Geography

North Guwahati is a historical important place, but to know the history of this area we have to trace a brief history of Assam as well as Kamrup as a whole.

History of Assam

Assam is a state situated in the north eastern part of India surrounded by other administrative units of the region, namely: Arunachal, Nagaland, Manipur, Mizoram, Tripura and Meghalaya and also by foreign countries like Bhutan and Bangladesh. In ancient times Assam constituted a part of the country known as Pragjyotisha and also Kamrupa. Mention of Pragjyotisha is found in the great epics, the Mahabharata and the Ramayana and also in some of the Puranas. However, the Pragjyotisha as mentioned in the epics was a much larger country. In the Mahabharata it is mentioned that the boundary of Pragjyotisha extended up to the Bay of Bengal in the south and Karatowa River in the west. From the *Sabha Parva* of the Mahabharata it is learnt that the army of Bhagadatta, the king of Pragjyotisha, consisted of Kiratas, Chinas and many other warriors dwelling in the coast of the sea, suggesting the fact that the territory of Bhagadatta reached the sea-shore. The Ramayana tells that the western boundary was formed by the river Koshi in Purnia District of modern Bihar. Some parts of Nepal and Bhutan were also included within the territory of ancient Pragjyotisha.

From the 4th century AD we have clear picture of the history of Assam. Yuan Chang's travel accounts, Bana's Harshcharita and above all various land grants plates and epigraphs supply valuable historical material. From these we gather that Pusyavarmana of the Varmana dynasty ruled in Kamrupa in the 4th century AD and was followed by other kings of the same line till the 7th century when Bhaskarvarmana ruled as the last king. This dynasty is held to be the descendants of Narakasura, a great mythological king from Videha or north Bihar whose capital was Pragjyotishpur as the Mahabharata says. Confirmed accounts of political and cultural links established between Kamrupa and the rest of India are to be found in the history of this period. After the *Varmanas* we have three other dynasties which ruled Kamrupa, the first beginning with *Salastambha*, the second the *Palas* and the third the *Khenas*. It is during the rule of the *Khenas* that Mohammedan first invaded Assam. In the medieval times, Pragjyotisha came to be known as Kamrupa. In the Kalika Purana, written in the 10th century AD, it has been stated that soon after Naraka of Mithila ascended the throne, the name Pragjyotisha was changed to Kamrupa. But Rajshekhar, a poet of the royal court of Mahipal, the king of Kannauj while describing aryavarta referred to Pragjyotisha and not to Kamrupa (Das 1968: 3-5). On the other hand Alberuni, who during the 11th century AD accompanied Sultan Mahmud to India mentioned the name of Kamrupa while dealing with eastern India.

Again, Hiuen Tsiang, a Chinese pilgrim who came to Kamrupa during the reign of Bhaskarvarmana in the 7th century AD, mentioned that to enter Kamrupa (Kia-no-leu-po) he had to cross a large river called Karatowa. He gave a very good account of Kamrupa. Thus, perhaps it can be said that till the 12th century AD, both the names, Kamrupa and Pragjyotisha were used indiscriminately to refer to almost the same country. But it must be kept in mind that the political boundary of ancient Pragjyotisha as well as Kamrupa was changed during different periods.

After the fall of the *Khens*, the *Koches* rose to power in about 1515 AD, but by that time the *Ahoms* were also expanding their rule from the east. The *Chutiyas* were ruling in the extreme north east, the *Kacharis* in mid Assam and in between them a number of petty chieftains called '*Bhuyans*" were holding sway over the Brahmaputra plains. Towards the close of the 18th century AD, the *Ahoms* began to disintegrate owing to internal strives born of misrule. In 1816 thousands of Burmese troops mounted an attack on Assam. They were invited by Badan Barphukan, the *Ahom* Governor at Guwahati. Owing partly to them *Ahom* kings misbehaviour and partly to lure of easy loot and plunder, the Burmese hordes came again in 1819 and for the third time in 1821 for the same reasons. They virtually ruled all over Assam from 1819 to 1824, killing people ruthlessly, plundering their property, burning villages, thus reducing the country to ruins and the whole social system to shambles, when the Burmese clashed with the British in Goalpara, they were driven back with superior weapons and better battle tactics and finally crushed and defeated, leading to the Treaty of Yandabu in 1826, by which the Burmese king gave away Assam to the British. Assam was the last territory of so called British India to go to them. That is why an Assamese poet refers Assam as the 'youngest daughter of Bharat'.

History of North Guwahati

North Guwahati was important place during the days of Narakasura and Bhagadatta, who was killed in the famous battle of Mahabharata. North Guwahati was the capital of *Dharampala*, one of the ruler of *Pala* dynasty in the name of *'Kamrup Nagar'*. The *Koch* king

Parikshit Narayan established his capital here and named it *'Durjay Nagar'*. The *'Parikshit pukhuri'* and *'Konwari Pukhuri'* at Shilsako tell the old tales of Koch dynasty. The Ahoms after sub-duing the Koch rulers in 1625 AD occupied the city and since then north Guwahati received care and patronage for its growth. The rulers confined their strategic installations within the south bank and shifted the administrative outpost to Rajaduar on the north bank. Since then north Guwahati served as the imperial gateway for further expansion of Ahom kingdom. North Guwahati hence attained the status of an administrative seat which promoted residential and other associated activities. North Guwahati was made administrative seat also because of its natural fortifications which still prevails.

The name north Guwahati has been used during the reign of Ahom kings when Barphukan and Paniphukan, the two royal Generals ruled over it. Till the advent of Britishers, north Guwahati was more important than the southern part. When the British established the capital of Assam in Shillong (present capital of Meghalaya), the importance gradually shifted to southern part leaving north Guwahati a heap of old historical and mythological ruins.

For war strategy, north Guwahati was the best place and has been proved on many occasions. In the past every battle fought here was won. The famous battle of Saraighat was fought here in north Guwahati under the Generalship of patriot Lachit Barphukan with Ramsingha, the Mughal General of repute. Again, Syed Chena and Sayed Firoz, the two Generals were defeated by Assamese soldiers here. Bokhtiar Khilizi was also defeated here. The famous stone inscription-*'kanai barashi boa'* describe all these facts in crude Assamese script – 'Rudra Singh, the Ahom king encamped here with a large army to invade north Bengal but unfortunately he died of severe attack of small pox and the whole mission was defeated.

Historian Kanaklal Barua (Barua, 1992: 14) assumes that the capital named *'Kamrup nagar'*, the city of Kamrud of the Muslim chroniclers, was at north Guwahati near the temple of Aswaklanta. The *Kamrupar Buranji* mentions the tradition that a king named Dharampala had his seat of government there. The modern town of north Guwahati possesses temples, roads, bridges, fortifications and moats which are clearly pre *Ahom* origin. There are two temples on the *Aswaklanta* hill. The upper temple contains the image of Vishnu lying on *Ananta Sajya*. It is one of the finest specimens of sculptural skill in Kamrupa about the beginning of the 12th century. The western part of the town is called *Shilsako*, because it still contains a small stone built bridge over a stream. The eastern part is known as Rajaduar (king's gate), which shows that the Raja's palace was there. The second copper plate of Dharampala was actually found in the village of Rangmahal about two miles to the north of Rajaduar. This is another indication that the capital was then at north Guwahati.

Composition of communities

North Guwahati is the resident of people of Assam. By people of Assam means whose mother tongue is Assamese and the indigenous tribal inhabitants of the state.

Assam is the homeland of several tribes – Rabha, Boro, Kachari, Karbi, Tiwa, Mishing etc. each of these has its own language. These people have migrated to Assam long ago and perhaps they were not called by the above names at that time. They had their own culture including language and physical characters. But in course of time due to different factors changes took place and they became Assamese or they had been Assamized (Das, 1968: 5). Hence, these people are undoubtedly a part of the people of Assam. People of Assam again include the caste population who are of Indo-Aryan origin and speak Assamese language. Mention should be made of that group of people of Assam who had come to Assam for economic reason during British rule, they are the tea garden labours and resident of Mymenshing District of then East Bengal.

Though the territory is a multi caste society yet there is no caste discrimination among the population. The traditional caste occupation found in the caste system of India is not prevalent here. People have received higher education and accordingly engage with different occupations as suitable for them.

Life style

Food and Drinks

A common practice noticed is the eating and chewing of *Tamol* (areca nut), both ripe and unripe, together with betel leaf and lime and sometimes with tobacco leaves. In India, the custom of chewing unripe betel nut exists only in Assam, this has been recorded both in the Harsacarita as well as in the accounts of the Mohammedan historians. The *fathiya –I – Ibriyah* states the people of Assam ate pan in large quantities with unripe supari, unshelled. The Yogini Tantra says that the women of Assam would always be chewing betel nut – *tambulasah sada bhavet.* Areca nut and betel leaf – *tamol-pan* as they are called in Assamese have a definite place in all the socio religious and ceremonial functions. In old days to receive a *tamol-pan* from the royal court is a great honour. Even today, in every household, first thing offered to a guest is *tamol-pan*. Time and distance are still now computed by the village people by the interval required to chew a nut.

Dress and ornaments

The textile material of ancient Assam as described in Kalika Purana include four classes – *karpasa* (cotton), *kambala* (wool), *balka* (bark) and *kosaja* (silk from cocoons).

Ksauma was a variety of cloth made of atasi fibre. *Ksauma* clothes are described in epics as 'pure as the autumn moon's light'. *Dukula* was the usual name for the finest *ksauma.* In the Royal Treasury chapter of Arthasastra mention has been made of the places of manufacture of this kinds of *Dukula*. It states that *Dukula* that was produced in *Survarnakudya* (Assam) was 'as red as the sun, as soft as the surface of the gem, woven while the threads were very wet and of uniform or mixed texture' (Barua, 1951: 145) and was considered as best. It is therefore evident that Assam even in the 4th cent.AD was celebrated for *Dukula* fit to be kept in the Royal Treasury. The Kalika Purana refers to hemp cloth (*sanavastram*) which was probably worn by ordinary people. The use of hemp fabrics is also known from the account of Hiuen Tsiang.

Kosaja or *kauseya* seems to be the silk obtained from the cocoons of various kinds of silk worms. The silks of Assam is derived from the two species of worms: *eri* or *endi* (Attacus ricini) and *muga* (Antheroea Assamoea). The *eri* cloth is of a drab colour and course in texture and is very durable. It is light but warm. The *muga* silk worm the scientific name of which trace connection with Assam is unique to this area. It is not found in any parts of India except Dehra Dun, where it occurs sparingly. There is a variety of *muga* called *campa muga*, its worm feeds on the leaves of the *campa* tree (Michelia champaka). Another kinds of *muga* known as *Mejankari*, the worm feeding on *Mejankari* or *Adakari* trees (Tetranthera polyantha). The *Mejankari* silk constitute the dress of the higher ranks, most of it being dyed red with lack. True silk, the modern Assamese white *pat* silk is called *patta* and is the product of Bombyx textor and Bombyx croesi, which feed on mulberry trees. In the Harsacarita, reference is made to sacks woven out of *pattasụtra* (silk yarns).

The art of dyeing both yarn and cloth was well known and four primary colours, namely, white, red, yellow and black or blue were recognized. Embroidered cloth was also manufactured and the gift of such clothes to God and Goddesses was considered meritorious.

In ancient Assam garments used were known as vastras or *acchadana* and were used in both forms, uncut and tailored or stiched (*Sucividdham*). The dress of men as revealed in the sculptures also consisted of a single unstitched undergarment (*paridhana*) like the present day *dhoti*. This was worn wrapped round the waist and hardly reached below the knee. It was held tight at the waist by a girdle (*parivesa*) consisting of three or more bands, fastened together by means of a knot in the centre, just below the naval. Sometimes one end of the garment was allowed to hang in graceful folds in the front. The use of *parivesa*, waist band is also known. Besides, the people of higher social status dressed in upper robes also known as *uttariya* and *uttariyasanga*. Women too appear to have worn two garments, the upper and the lower. The lower garment descended from the stomach to the ankles, it is called *mekhela*. It is a sort of petticoat in the form of an elongated sack open at both ends. It is worn by adjusting it either above the breast or round the waist. When adjusted round the waist the *mekhela* reaches to the ankles. Aged women or in ceremonious occasion *riha* is worn by wrapping round the waist. Over the *riha* is placed a kind of shawl known as chadar. The male and females sometimes used *'kanchuki'* to cover their upper part, as known from ancient sculptures. The males of distinctive status used headdresses called *ushnisha* (*Paguri*). This practice is still found among the villagers.

In Assamese common term used for cloth is *kapor*, which is believed to be a variation of Sanskrit term *karpata*. At present, Sualkuchi is the most important centre for weaving traditional Assamese textiles. It is 30 km drive from north Guwahati, which still preserves the tradition of weaving *muga* and *pat* silk of Assam. However, common people still prefers cotton clothes than silk one for their day to day utility. Here to be mentioned that though the textiles of Assam bear an age old tradition, yet in due course of time, the techniques of weaving has changed a lot. Use of scientific machines and techniques have reduced the use of traditional handlooms. Changes in motifs and designs have occurred too. Likewise dressing style has changed to far extent. Girls from younger generation wear modern dresses. Likewise male wear shirts and trousers stitched in modern fashion, only limited aged one wear *dhooti* and *kurta*. The turban has now been remained only with religious occasions. But, married women usually keep their head covered with their *chadar* and in ceremonial occasions specially in marriage and religious functions, along with women unmarried girls also wear *mekhela chadar*, which is almost has become compulsion. In normal day to day activities *saree* is also seen wearing.

Ornaments are often worn by women. For a married woman *sindur* is must along with other ornaments like necklace, earings, bangle etc. *Mangal Sutra* is not compulsory like north Indian married women. Gold is most common.

Education

Concern for education is very apparent among the people of north Guwahati as a whole. The town has the priviledge of producing many nobles of Assam in different fields. The first ICS and 5th in the chronology of Indian ICS and also second Indian ICS to have the independent charge of the district during *'British Raj'*, the great scholar Anundo Ram Boruah was born here. He was a great scholar of Sanskrit. Karmabir Nabin Ch. Bardoloi was the first Assamese leader who led the Assam deputation to England to pled for Governor Province status for Assam during the days of Montagu-Chelsford Reform in respect of provinces in India in 1918. Late Lakhiram Barooah was the first Acharya in classical music in Assam. Shri Jyotirmoy Barooah, the first Assamese Indian Deputy High Commissioner is from north Guwahati. Shri Sarat Das, a north Guwahatian is the first Assamese footballer to captain the famous Mohun Bugan team for several years. The first Assamese female President of Asom Sahitya Sabha Late Nalinibalal Devi was also from North Guwahati.

Thus the concern for education has always remain priority for the people of north Guwahati. There is clear emphasis for the education of the young generations. Factors like household chores and caste does not form barrier in pursuing formal education. Uneducated parents also seemed keen in sending their children to school. Some students are seen going for private tutorials to aid them in their class studies.

There are several schools (both primary and secondary and both Assamese and English medium). The Faculty Higher Secondary in north Guwahati is one of the best schools of Assam. Children from nearby villages also study in these schools. Inspite of being mulit caste society, there is no apparent caste discrimination in the field of education. Further there is no gender discrimination as well. Girls have higher percentage in class and they are more active in extra curricular activities than boys. For higher education there is North Guwahati College, which has produced several distinguished personalities of the society.

Religion and Festivals

The importance of religion in north Guwahati can be gauged from the fact that it is also known as 'kashi of the east'. Religion occupies center stage in the life of people. The presence of it is felt in virtually every aspect of village social life. People are followers of Hinduism. A few Muslim families are there in nearby villages, who are living here for several generations. Both Vaishnavism and saivism is followed here, where as vaishnavism is pre dominant.

Annual religious festival cycle includes many festivals celebrated at different levels. A look into the religious calendar of the village gives the necessary insight into this domain.

There are several temples and *Namghars* (vaishnava temple) in the villages. *Namghar* literally means the house of namas. It is a simple structure where the vaishnavite Hindus or Assamese recite the name of God. *Namgharars* were introduced in Assam by the vaishnavite saint Sankaradeva.

But the main center is the Doul Govinda temple, which draws devotees of far distance. The temple plays a pivotal role in the life of the villagers. In spite of the prevalence of two sects – vaishnavism and saivism, there is no religious obligations among the villagers and they participate the ceremonies of each other. Thus, religion seems to be inextricably linked to peoples lives.

Economy

The economy of people of Rajaduar, Madhyamkhanda and Shilsako was agro based during Britishers or post independence era. People used to cultivate either in their own land or the land holders acquired during *'Brtish Raj'*. During the same period few officials were also there such as *tehsildars*, *Sadar Amin*, Judges along with a few service holders in clerical cadre. After independence, specially with the introduction of land reform policy, the economy of the people had undergone drastic changes. Weaving was a good supplement in agricultural income. Even today, lace making handloom cottage industry is a good source of income to many families. At present every eight to ten families have a service holder. Every family have their own kitchen garden and at least one milch cow. Industry does not grow here due to communication problem, but changes taking place gradually, specially after the Indian Institute of Technology (IIT) Guwahati chapter has started. Business does not flourish here due to lack of wide marketing scope. Most of the people have to cross to the south bank every day and get their shopping done there. Because of such situation, north Guwahati still shows less progress as compared to south bank. It is quite interesting that an area close to Guwahati, which has become metropolitan city and the main center for north east India, still shows such slow progress. However, changes taking place in several sectors, urbanization gradually influencing north Guwahati.

Doul Govinda as Sacred Complex

The Doul Govinda as a sacred complex is one of the criteria within the ambit of the concept of eco museum. Here, Doul Govinda has been studied as a center of pilgrimage. It has been examined as an integrated institution of Assamese ethnic heritage. My endevour is to bring into focus the interconnections of different groups of people who are part of the institution and to find out how these interactions resulted the significant tangible and intangible heritage of the territory. It is important to understand the social organization of the sacred complex within the eco museum parameters. In Doul Govinda sacred complex there are three lairs of people who are part of the social organization that makes a network for all the activities that takes place not only at the sacred complex itself but also in the entire territory.

In the eco museum concept one of the parameters identified by the Museologists is the territory. Now territory here is intimately connected with the local identity. The local identity is signified by a distinct institution and the institution may be of varied nature, but in Indian context sacred complexes have been recognized as the prime institution giving identity to a territory.

There are Anthropological studies on sacred complexes which reveals the advantages of a particular territory to become a museum without wall, because of the tangible and intangible heritages connected with the sacred complex as well as voluntary association of the people with the complex. The focus of study hence on these conceptual aspects of new museology in the given territory.

A Note on Sacred Complex

The theory of sacred complex dates back to the mid fifties of the 20th century when under the influence of Chicago School of Anthropology, Prof L. P. Vidyarthi studied the pilgrimage town of Gaya, located in the ancient cultural zone of Magadh. Although he attempted to study that sacred city as a dimension of Indian civilization yet he took some time to refine and modify several analytical concepts of sacred complex in connection with the study of Gaya . He tried to prove the hypothesis that the sacred specialist of a Hindu place of pilgrimage is intimately connected with the level of continuity, compromise and combination between great and little tradition. The sacred specialist of a place of pilgrimage maintain a distinct way of life and are responsible for the transition of certain elements of the great tradition to the folk tradition by popularizing certain texts as the grassroots level and by organizing pilgrimage and by officiating as the temple priests. The sacred complex in general and the sacred specialists in particular, have been in the process of modification and transformation as a great development in the larger universe of Hindu civilization of which they are a part.

In the study of "Sacred complex of Hindu Gaya "several terms were used by Vidyarthi such as "Sacred cluster'', "Sacred segment" and "Sacred zone" to describe the sacred centers constituting the sacred geography of Gaya, "local", "regional" and "universal" to indicate the scope of some of the element of the sacred complex and "folk",

"Sanskritic", "feudalistic" and "proletarian" to describe the nature of the priesthood. These terms provide a typology for describing the pattern of sacred complex (Vidyarthi et.el, 1979: 12). It is important to understand such terms as they give a local identity to a sacred complex.

The main finding of the study of Gaya was that the Sacred Complex in Hindu Gaya is based on trichotomic inter-related phenomena , viz. the sacred geography, the sacred performance the sacred specialists. The complex network of relationship which connects Hindu Gaya with other centers and region of the India was also brought into light (Vidyarthi et.el, 1979: 12). Here we notice the significance of the ecology, community and the intangible heritage of a given territory.

Although there were some historical description of Hindu places of pilgrimage by Indologists, Orientalists and Travelers before the middle of 20th century, it was not until the early 1950's that the cultural analysis of these places began to appear. Gaya was perhaps the first to attract the attention of Anthropology (Vidyarthi et.el, 1979: 12-13). Although Redfield's concept of civilization as a complex structure of great and little traditions and his collaborator Milton Singer while studying the city of Madras used several words viz. "Cultural Center", "Cultural performance", "Cultural specialists" etc. but these terms were so broad – based and comprehensive that the researcher had to modify them in the study of Hindu place of pilgrimage. In this connection, Vidyarthi first of all modified these terms and concepts and gave definition of several words, which are now used by the Anthropologist in the study of Hindu places of pilgrims as dimension of Indian civilization, while defining a 'sacred center' he said "sacred center'' represents a single spot where a sacred performance take place (Vidyarthi , 1961: 32). Thus according to him a sacred center is the smallest unit of worship. A bigger unit then the sacred center is the "sacred cluster" and when there are number of sacred center in and around one place, it has been termed as "sacred cluster "by him . He also pointed out that in a sacred cluster where there are a number of sacred centers, the forms of worship is usually modified according to the dominated sacred centers, however, there may be a notable exceptions. The sacred cluster and the sacred centre could be viewed from the parameters of the 'headquarter' and 'antenna' within the eco museum concept.

When two or more clusters at the place of pilgrimage form a continuous segment it has been defined as "sacred segment" and different sacred segments of a place pilgrimage constitute the sacred geography of the land. In this way several words were used by Vidyarthi to describe the sacred centers particularly from organization point of view.

Similarly he suggested that all those rites and rituals, which are performed at a sacred center, might be called "sacred performance". The sacred performance may vary from simple *japa,* recitation of God's name to *artis* and complicated form of *yogna, havens* and *upachar* worship.

Thus all rituals and devotional activities, which are performed at a sacred center, may be called "Sacred performanc". The same activities had been also referred to by Milton Singer as "cultural performance" but he used it in a very broader context. For instance, all cultural activities or cultural performances are not sacred, for the word "culture" has a very broad meaning in Anthropology and thus in the context of studying a Hindu place of pilgrimage, Vidyarthi used "sacred performance" in the religious context as well as some restricted sense of its application. The sacred performance is the intangible heritage of a community, which at times based on collective memory of the sacred specialists.

In the study of sacred centers and sacred performance we come across several types of "sacred specialist" and while defining them Vidyarthi said "those persons who earn wholly or partially, by some kind of religious services" may be called "sacred specialists" (Vidyarthi et.el, 1979: 13) Thus under this category various persons are included irrespective of caste and sect considerations, ranging from priests and *pandits* to palmists, devotional singers, reciters of *katha*, *puranas*, musicians, barbers, shopkeepers, selling the sacred ingredients etc., although their involvements person to person and at place to place . This network of the specialists highlights the cultural interaction in the given territory that makes it distinct from other places.

Thus in the study of Hindu Gaya,. Vidyarthi used three analytical concepts viz., a "sacred geography", "sacred performance" and "sacred specialists" and according to him "these three concepts conceived collectively are termed as sacred complex" (Vidyarthi , 1961: 111 – 113). In this was the "sacred complex of Hindu Gaya" studied as the dimension of Indian civilization introduced a new field of investigation in Indian Anthropology.

At the applied level, the study of sacred complex helps us to understand the problems related to Indian civilization. It also examines the question of change in traditional Indian culture. Thus at the applied level, it unfold the traditional channels of civilization integration and helps to know the various facts of unity and diversity in Indian civilization. In India there are number of geographical regions, there are number of linguistic zones, people belong to various caste and creed, they believe in different faith and sects and are of different political temperament and thus we find that there are various diversities in Indian culture civilization. But through the institution of pilgrimage people overcome these diversities and thus establish unity in Indian culture and civilization and that is why we find that irrespective of geographical, linguistic, economic and political barriers, people visit the sacred centers all over the country. These modes of unity and diversity in Indian culture and civilization are amply demonstrated in the study of the sacred complex. In this way we find that the study of sacred complex has both academic and applied value and further researches carried out in this direction will bring new facts of Indian civilization.

It is not enough to explain the phenomena of sacred complex in a much wider civilization context on the basis of the works so far been made on the same. In most of the works the general trend has been to examine to their organizational frame and socio-religious functions. However it is prominently that some of the phenomena observed at Gaya were found in other sacred centers also, although certain regional variation in the sacred performances as well as the organization of the sacred specialists have also been noticed.

Finally, considered from the methodological point of view , the concept of sacred complex as formulated and developed by Prof. Vidyarthi , is not only widely applicable to the *Pauranic Trithas* of the Hindu universe , but it has also become an important theme in the study of both the complex and primitive societies in India as dimension of India civilization . Each analytical element of the sacred complex is formed on both textual and scriptural canons and exists at the contextual level and both are upheld by creation, perpetuation and continuous tradition of sacred myths. These sacred myths, when examined from the point of view of process of transmission, acquire omnibus character and absorb varieties of textual and oral traditions in time and space. Thus, methodologically, the study of sacred complex of a Hindu place pilgrimage, also unfolds, in addition to many other matters of theoretical importance, channels of transmission in the integration of civilization.

The Doul Govinda Temple

The advent

The Lord Govinda is enshrined in North Guwahati, across the Brahmaputra river where one can experience the remains of various wars, incidents and monuments, in other words an unprotected open-air museum. The history of the seat of Lord Doul Govinda, in this historic place is equally stunning and interesting.

To trace the history of Lord Doul Govinda, one has to go back to 1826 A.D. On 24th February of this year is also important for the famous Iyandabu resolution, through which, Assam lost its independence and the British rule began . It was the policy of the Britishers to incorporate the local elite class of the society in their reign. Likewise Ganga Ram Barua was appointed as Sub-Divisional Head of the Nalbari area, who was the father of the brainchild of Assam Anando Ram Barua, the first Assamese to hold the post of I.C.S. under the British rule.

During his tenure one strange happened in a village called Jakeria, near the Rangia town. One cow of a Brahmin, always at dawn, freeing herself of the cowshed where her owner used to rope her at night noticed to have gone to the nearest forest called *Sandhyajar* and starts emitting milk spontaneously after reaching a particular grass bush of *Birina*. After milking, she always would come back quietly to her shed. Hearing this strange news, the Sub Divisional Officer (S.D.O) one day reached there to witness the incident with his own. To dispel all misgivings and rumours, the place was dug up and around 4 ft. underneath a surprisingly magnificent idol of Lord Krishna playing flute was discovered.

An account can be recorded here from *'Dandua-Droh'*- a novel by famous Novelist of Assam, Rajanikanta Bardaloi who functioned as Magistrate in-charge of land settlement in Rongia area, indicated the existence of the village Jakeria in the same woods of Sandhyajar where Hara Dutta and Veera Dutta had their *Haveli*. These two brothers rose in rebellion against the Ahom hegemony and declared independence whereupon men of the Ahom Governor Barphukan Kaliya Bhomora of Guwahati chased and vanquished them. They were caught and slained later on. This rebillion took place during the period of 1788-1795 AD. This was the era of fall of Ahom kingdom and several such rebillions were recorded from small Princely States. It is believed that before the Hara Dutta fled his village, he kept their family deity hidden under the ground at the village Jakeria. The village later turned into jungles and named Sandhyajar. There are lots of possibilities that the idol of Lord Krishna found during Garga Ram Baruah Sadar Amin was the same one that was kept hidden underground by Hara Dutta. However, an authentic link yet to be established upon this account.

With the consent of general public the idol was given great reverence and ceremonious welcome in the Namghar of Rajaduar-the native village of the S.D.O. For the better well being and maintenance of the idol, the S.D.O. approached his Guru Shree Brindaban Chandra Ata, who was taking shelter at that time in Kurua and advised him to install and worship the idol in the village Namghar. That is how; the idol was set along the time of Shri Shyamrai idol, who was being worshipped there for a long time. Meanwhile the annual Holi festival was approaching in the month of *Falguna* and the members were in great dilemma because till then original Namghar deity had been the image of Lord Shyam Rai another form of Lord Shri Krishna and was unable to decide as to which of the two deities they should place on the *Doul* during the Holi festival. It is said that the priest prayed and left the decision to be indicated by the two deities for resolution of the impasse and to his surprise, the priest found on the following morning the new image of Lord Krishna to have taken stand as few inches ahead of the image of Lord Shyam Rai on the altar. The priest and members of the *Namghar* had no difficulty in deciding the preference and they accordingly installed the new image of Lord Shri Krishna on the *Doul* an outhouse temple at the courtyard of the *Namghar* for celebrating the Holi festival, since then, the new image of Lord Shri Krishna came to be recognized as Lord Doul Govinda. After some time, the image of Lord Shyam Rai fell down from the throne of the *Namghar* and lost one hand. Thus, the idol of Lord Shyam Rai got itself removed from the sanctum of the temple.

The Temple Premises

The temple premises a place of divine bliss are of recent construction started during 1970's with the donations and contributions from devotees. Presently the project for construction of devotees rest house has been taken up near the mandir premises. The location of the *mandir*, the *Doul* and the two open halls with other adjunct sheds is on a strip of high land cut out and leveled on the northern slope of the Chandra Bharoti hillock. Whereas the main *mandir*, the sanctum and the open hall in the front and the *Douls* to the eastern side are all concrete structures, the second open hall in front of the *Doul* is of Assam type roof. The *Bat-chora* (i.e. the gate) and the entire Mandir premises present a graceful look to any visitor bringing about a serene atmosphere to the locality. The campus is a well-laid-out project of the public of Rajaduar in collaboration of other devotees of the neighbouring areas. People have the faith that all these new constructions in place of the old *Namghar, Monikut* and *Doul* have come to being with the grace of Lord Doul Govinda.

Every morning devotees congregate in the temple premises and wait a long queue to offer obeisance to the deity at the sanctum sanctorum. Such congregations reach peak size, swelling into several thousands in number, during winter months of *Magh* and *Fagun* (mid Jan – mid March) and also in the beginning of the year in *Baishakh* (mid April – mid May). Blissful devotion (*Bhakti-rasa*) pervades the place sanctifying every soul that comes here. All worldly carvings get sublimated in human heart with total surrender at the feet of the Lord Doul Govinda. Devotees are attracted to this shrine at Rajaduar from all directions. Some come by road and others crossing the Brahmaputra from the south bank by ferry service or engine-fitted boats.

Vaishnavism : the Organizing Principle

The Doul Govinda temple is a medieval temple where neo vaishnavism is followed. In Assam, this trend was introduced by Srimanta Sankardeva in 16th century. In below a brief of Sankradeva and his contribution to the socio-religious life of the people of Assam has been discussed.

Sankardeva is regarded as the foremost religious preceptor of a large reformers of Assam in the middle ages - the age of socio-religious reformation.

Sankardeva was born in 1449 in the village of Bordowa in Central Assam. His father was chieftain or *Bara Bhuyan*. By the time Sankaradeva was born, the *Bhuyans* had lost their semi royal power to the rising Ahom power and had become a part of the land holding class.

Early in life, Sankardeva was puzzled by the inconsistencies of the *Sakta* religion, which was prevalent in Assam at that time. *Saktas* are worshippers of the Hindu God Siva and Goddess *Shakti* or *Durga. Saktas* priests were considered to be physically and spiritually tyrannical by the common man.

Sankardeva spent a large part of his life traveling different parts of India. When he returned to Assam after his first long trip extending over twelve years, he started a religious movement based on the "*Bhagavad-Gita*". Sakardeva made the Gita his scripture and Krishna, the heroic incarnation of Vishnu, his God. The Bhagavad or *Ek Sarana Nama Dharma* (only one God religion), espoused by Sankardeva in Assam in contemporary to other religious movement took place in different parts of Indian subcontinent. This movement of simplification in religious beliefs, also called the '*Bhakti movement*' where one is guided by one's devotion and adoration(or *bhakti*) to a divine .

Sankardeva shunned priests in all religious services and ceremonies. He preached against the use of idols during prayers. He invited all castes, races and religions to his prayer services. He taught that all human beings are children of Vishnu, possess immortal souls and are hence equal in their dignity. He conducted religious services in *Namghars*.

Philosophy

Sankaradeva's philosophy is based on *Dasya Bhakti*. Krishna is taken as Lord and disciple as servant. It is through this way of life, the path to reach the creator was preached (Neog, 1967: 33). The love for Krishna as Sankaradeva has said.

"*Advaitavada and visista daitvavada slokadhena prabhakishami yaduktang granthakotibhib Brahma satya jagannmithya jeeva kevalam*".

The interpretation of the above verse is as follows:

Brahma is true and to get Brahma there is specific way. I shall to take the help of *Avataras*. Krishna is that *Avatara* through whom we have the knowledge of Brahma. Brahma is true for the world is false, as the soul is the creator.

Srimanta Sankaradeva found a link to reach the creator that is through devotion and self surrender to Lord Krishna. The difference between the absolute self and individual self is finally brought out by him in his noted treatise *"Bhaktiratnakara"*. The individual soul can only shake off *maya* only through devotion to *Hari bhakti*. The causes of *mayavandha* are many. In enjoying worldly pleasures and doing all *karmas* the individual soul gets tied up with the world and enjoys pleasure and pain accordingly. Besides taking sole refuge in God for attaining the sate of detachment from the world and salvation. *Joga – Buddhist* philosophy *of Sanyama* is emphasized in Sankaradeva's said work as well as in his *'Anadi-patana'*. Sankaradeva stressed in *karma* and *jnyana*. There should be *bhakti* – the teaching that resembles 'Gita' too (Neog, 1967: 36).

As in the " *Kali Yuga* " *bhakti* based on the name of Hari, known by the many names Krishna , Narayana etc.. This is the best way to shake off Maya and to attain salvation. This creed became known as "*Eka Sarana Nama Dharma*". In fact Narayana, the eternal reality is the creator, sustainer and destroyer of the universe, through *maya*, Sankaradeva in Kirttana states:

" *Tumise kewala sara, sarbe mayamaya* |
Tomatese hante srishti howe sthiti laya ||
Jagata karana niranjana satyabadi |
Jara mayapesi ito samsara nirmana ||

Sri Sankaradeva in " *Ek sarana bhakti*" formulated *bhakti* in a style to awaken the devotion. Which is selfless in nature. Sankaradeva in his works has repeatedly said :

" *Ramayate iti Rama* "

(One who becomes a source of pleasure himself becomes a source of pleasure to Brahma)

Sankaradeva showed to the disciples the way to *Vaikuntha* through a very simple devotion of taking refuge at the feet of ones formless God (*Nirakara*) and made them recognize the four pillars of Bhagvata Bhakti , viz ,*"guru"*, *"deva"*, *"nama" and "bhakta"*.

"SAKARDEVE O PUNORUPATI DEKHAILANTA
GURU DEVA NAMA BHAKTA SAINAI DILANTA"

Sankaradeva's Contribution

Language

Language is an important mode to translate one's thoughts and Sri Sankaradeva picked up the spoken dialect of the masses , added luster and sacredness to it as he used it in writing the *Bargits* and *Ankiya natas* . The twelve pilgrimage in Northern India, was the banking ground for his formative adaptation of the local dialect. Then impact of Vidyapati's Brajawali songs and his witnessing of some social performances combined with the direct experience and intermingling with the local people appears to have helped him in developing the script and dialect .

In his various writings, Sankaradeva seems to use three types of language, such as 1. literary Assamese 2. Colloquial Assamese and 3. Brajawali. Saint Sankaradeva used *Brajawali* in his *Bargits* and *Ankiya natas*, whereas he wrote and translated other books in standard Assamese except the *"Bhakti–Ratnakara"* in Sanskrit. Simulataneously we find some sort of colloquial speech in dialogues of certain characters in his *"Parijat harana nata*". Thus Sankaradeva seems to be familiar with varieties of speeches current in his time , through which he created a new organized form. These are none but *"dulari"*, *"payara*", *"jhumuri"*, *"jhamak"*, *"Git"*, *"Bhatima"*, *"Bargit"*, *" Tala-mana-naca"*, *"Bhawana"* .

The term *Brajawali* is applied to such a language in which Vaishnava songs were compared in the regions, viz. , Braja , now Mithila , Bengal , Orissa and Nepal; but in Assam this sacred language is called *Brajawali*. It is worth observing that saint Madhavadeva, the principal disciple of Saint Sankardeva, termed this peculiar language as *Brajawali* (Neog, 1967: 49).

The following dialect highlights the use of colloquial dialect by Sankaradeva :

Awe Pamari Sakhi ! Ohi Indraka dekhai atawe
Darppa kayeli,Aba tohari bhataraka kaiche
nahi palayata? Hamu manusi hoya tohari parijata niya jau
Oh! Tape marite najawa –

----- *Parijata Harana Nata* by Sankaradeva

This is piece of chattering –battle occurred between Satyabhama (the wife of Krishna) and Sashiprabha (the wife of Indra) for taking away the Parijat flower from latter's garden.

It is a credit to the genius of Saint Sankaradeva that he revived the Brajawali language through his *Bargits* and *Ankiya Natas* and inspired the Vaishnava devotees of Assam to continue it till the 18th century AD even after.

Literature

Culture is bed of roses for the mind. It is that powerful medium which provides man's mind the solace from traumas of life. Sankaradeva, through his poetry tried to awaken the dormant embryo of the mind of the masses. He effectively transforms the life of people. When he wrote plays and enacted them he involved different sections of society.

A very famous incident is narrated about the extraordinary capacity of Sri Sankaradeva. It is that Koch king Naranarayana desired the gist of Bhagavata. Accepting the challenge overnight he wrote it on a sachipat and presented it to the king, which is called *"Gunamala"*. Sankaradeva was not only indebted to the Bhagavata for its Krishna legends but also for literary forms, expressions and traditions. He translated the Bhagavata not only into Assamese words, but also into Assamese idioms (Neog, 1967: 51). Besides the translation he composed a large muber of other books with material from this *"Purana"*.

Kirttana

This is the first work of Sankaradeva written precisely for the purpose of propagating the faith. A "*Kirttana – Ghosa*" or simply a "*Kirttana*" is song for community singing consisting of two parts - a *Ghosa* is refraing and a number of *padas*. It is called *kirttana* (narration) as it is narrative in character and several *kirttanas* combine to make a story. Sankaradeva started composing *kirttanas* after he had heard the whole of the "*Bhagavata Purana*" explained to him by Jagadish Mishra.

The date of composition of the "*Kirttana*" is not known. Some biographers say that Sankaradeva did not write the book during one particular period and that the composition was spread over several years. According to Sankaradeva, there are 9 types of bhakti, viz, "*srawana*", "*kirttana*" , "*smarana*", "*arcana*" "*padasewana*", "*dasya*", "*sakhitwa*", "*bandana*" *and* "*deha-arpana*". Among these "*srawana*" *and* "*kirttana*" are the best. Therefore he wanted that his disciples should find him in the "*Kirttana-Ghosa*" itself.

"*Kirttana*" is not a single poem but a selective collection of twenty –six poems comprising about 2261 coupltes in diverse meters. Most of the poems are however adaptation from the "*Bhagavata Purana*". Two of its poem "*Sahasra nama brittanta*" *and* "*Ghunuca*" are written by two of his disciples Ananata Kandali, who in fact was the teacher that became disciple later on and Sidhartha Kandali and were incorporated is the anthology at the desire of the authors.

The very name "*Kirttana*" is suggestive of the fact that the poems were recited in religious congregations and services. Each poem bears a *ghosha* a refrain. These poems are recited by the leader of the religious gathering. After reading a couplet, the leader repeats the *ghosha* or refrain the party takes it up along with the clapping of hands. The first poem of the "*Kirttana*" *Chaturbimsati Avatara* (Twenty – four incarnations) describes briefly the twenty-four incarnations of God, making particular references to the divine personality of the Krishna *avatara* and to his activities liberation of mankind.

Nimi nawa sidha sambada

This book is a doctrinal treatise based on Book XI of the Bhagavata (*Nawa siddha katha ito ekadasa skandha*)

Anadi Patana

It is an account of cosmology and cosmogony, philosophy and theology.

Uttarakanda (Ramayana)

The *uttarakanda* (Ramayana) is in no sense an Assamese translation of Valmikis Ramayana, for Sankaradeva himself calls his work *'uttarakanda kathasara'*. Broadly speaking, it follows the course of Valmikis story, but the entire spirit of Sankaradeva's differs widely from that of the epic. He has omitted all the episodes not belonging to the main story, dismissed many chapters in a few lines, skipped over the rambling degressions that might have interfered with the continuity of his story. This is a unique and unparallel creation of Sankaradeva that is not to be found in any of the Ramayana of modern Indian languages

The Namghar

There are several temples and *Namghars* (vaishnava temple) in the villages. *Namghar* literally means the house of *namas*. It is a simple structure where the vaishnavite Hindus of Assam recite the name of God. *Namgharars* were introduced in Assam by the vaishnavite saint Sankaradeva.

Namghars primarily have two major spaces, the *monikut* (the sanctuary) and the assembly space. The direction of the principal axis of the *namghar* is always in east west direction. The *simhasana* or the altar is placed at the east facing west. Devotees sit facing the *simhasana* towards east. The monikut shelters the *simhasana*. The devotees play in the assembly space of the *namghar*. The *namghar's* architecture reflects its usage pattern, Assam's climatic conditions and the indigenous building materials. There are *namghars* in most of Hindu villages in Assam. In some areas such as Nagaon district, there is at least one, sometimes several public *namghars* in every village. The identity of the village folks in such places is tied closely to the *namghar* they attend. There is an ancient *namghar* called *kirttan ghar* in the town of Barpeta located in the Barpeta Satra.

The public *namghars* are not for every day use. They are places of assembly for special religious events and memorial services only. Private family *namghars* are like small private chapels. Sometimes there is an added assembly space, particular when it is attached to the residence of the *sattradhikar* the spiritual leader of the community. Apart from religious and memorial services, *namghars* serve as theatres for the performance of the indigenous art form, the *bhawana*. Spectators almost always overflowed the halls. Since this usually happens in the evening, rural *namghars* without electricity use lantens for illumination.

The public *namghar's* design is unique its assembly space is always very open, large, bright and airy. It is a response to the extremely humid, relatively mild temperatures and infrequent breezes during the most oppressive days. The roof is the primary feature, walls often being a bamboo screen and sometimes even non existent. Till a few decades ago, most rural *namghars* had thatched roofs over bamboo rafters and woven bamboo sheathing/sub roof. It is an elegant, cool, environment friendly and economically sustainable soulution. In the late 20th century most namghras have shed their thatched for tin roofs. This is despite the fact that tin roofs are hot, glary, noisy and lacks the friendly visual embellishments provided the natural bamboo rafters and woven sheathing (*sai*) topped by the tan and brown blades of dried grass roofing. Thatch roofing provided unusually high heat penetration resistance, probably the roofing with the highest R value, even today, aside from its beauty and appropiatness in the pastoral and lush green settings of Assam.

In earlier days the roof used to be supported by timber columns or bamboo poles although reinforced cement pillars are becoming common.

Rural Assam's indigenous builders/architects did not understand the concept of braced walls column supports. So often when the timber or bamboo poles buried in the soil rotted or got damaged by termites and other organisms the whole structure took the shape of rhombus with the onset of *Bardoisila* (the spring winds). It was a recurrent sign of disrepair and economic deprivation in rural Assam and still is. X-bracing with bamboo strips could extend the life of these leaning structures that remain. In early days, the floors almost always of mud. It used to be wiped before and after an event, by hard, with a rag mop and clay punning. Today's cement floors are an improvement. However, even today, a central longitudinal area in a *namghar* is kept unpaved with cement. This is the area where actors assemble during the performance of a *Bhawana*.

The *monikut* is a small structure hipped or gabled roof has either no windows or very little ones. This is the mysterious space. Children and those who are not privy are not allowed to venture into it. It was a space to be entered only by the *satradhikar* or other priviledged elders. The structure itself was no different from assembly hall, just smaller and darker to create a sense of veneration and mystery.

The other architectural element of the *namghars* is the *Ghai khuta*, the main pillar. It is usually an oversized column in the assembly hall. It is the second left facing north east from the entrance. The floor around this pillar is raised little. It is usually identified by a *gamosa* tied around it. No one is allowed to sit near this pillar as that is considered as the place of *Burha Dangaria* (a holy spirit). When in the *namghar* any *Mah Prasad* or offerings are distributed after a service, at first offering is made to that pillar as a custom. The pillar is also called *Lai Khuta*.

Sacred Geography

North Guwahati is a small town with panoramic beauty with a population of 25,000 (as per year 2000-01 census). The town is on the bank of the river Brahmaputra with several holy shrines all over. The significance of North Guwahati, within the ambit of sacred geography as postulated by Vidyarthi, could be seen from the network of sacred centers around it. First of all the Brahmaputra river, which is also considered as sacred as the river Ganga within that sacred geography making it more significant as territory parallel to the Doul Govinda on the south of bank of Brahmaputra is the Kamakhya on Nilachal hills – the *Shakti Pitha*. Towards east again on the south bank is the Navagraha temple another astrologically important site and other temple sites.

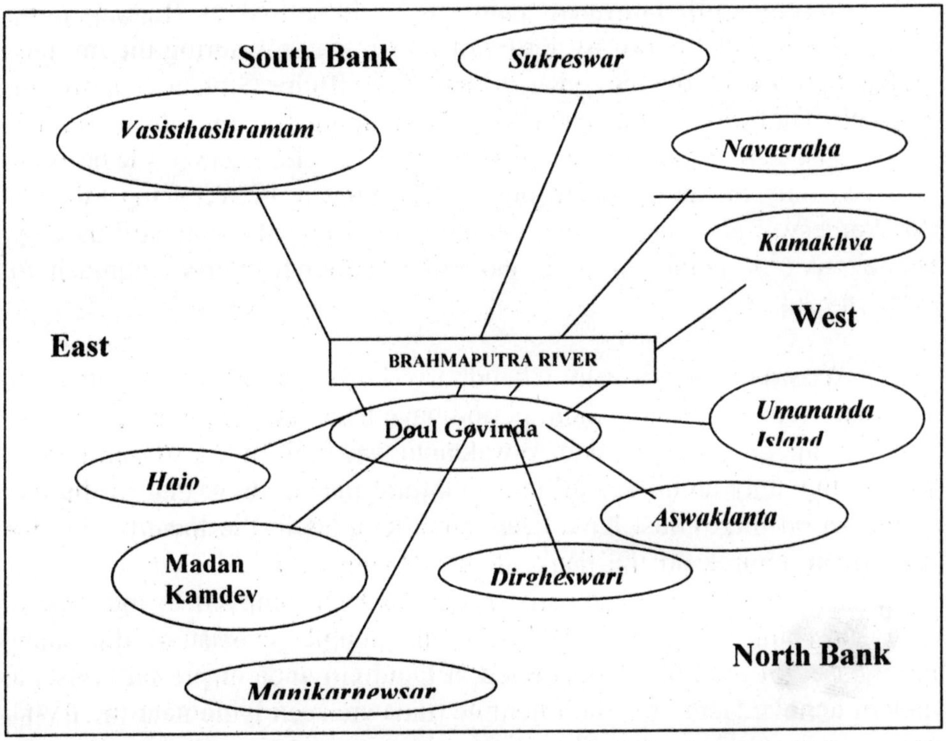

The human habitation of Rajaduar where the temple of Lord Doul Govinda is located is protected by an elongated stretch of highland named Chandra Bharati mound. It is believed that poet Anantakandali of Hajo who was also famous as poet Chandra Bharatti for his works '*Kumar Haran Kabya*' came here to participate in a symposium on the epic Mahabharata held at Umananda. This symposium is said to have been organized in honour of Maharaj Naranarayan, the great Koch king and poet Chandra Bharati was welcomed at this hillock at North Guwahati. The poet was overwhelmed by the beauty of nature all around, the interspersed green hills on both the north and south, channeling the Brahmaputra down to the west with shrines of Gods and Goddesses located in both the banks. All this made feel elated, it was unblemished joy for him.

Present north Guwahati came to be identified as Rajaduar, the king's gateway as the post of north Guwahati, perhaps during the military preparations made by the great Ahom king Rudra Singha against the Mughals. The king could reach the Brahmaputra for any naval journey from his pleasure house Rang mahal, about three kilometers to the north of the river, only by the pass cut out as the gateway between the hillocks Monikarneswar and chandra bharati *mandap*. This is the road still used by the devotees of Doul Govinda and other public for ferry approach to southern bank.

According to Dr. R.D. Choudhury (Barua, 1992: 12-14), at north Guwahati ruins of the pre Ahom period have been noticed in many places. Although the present temple at Aswaklanta was built in the Ahom period, the existing stray architectural and sculptural pieces show that in the pre Ahom period there must have been some temples in the locality. To the west of the temple on the bank of the Brahmaputra chiseled stones are noticed. A stone potika from this place has been removed to the Assam State Museum. The steps, leading to the temple, consist of the stone pieces, used in the pre Ahom period at Doul Govinda at present exists a modern temple. Here pre Ahom temple ruins are seen lying near the PWD road. Architectural remains like sila stambha, amolaka, potika etc. are seen in a state of disorder along with some images. As the nature of the ruins shows, there must have existed a Siva temple in 8th or 9th century. About 1 km west of the place on the PWD road itself, old stone blocks of various sizes, some bearing decorative designs and some chiseled marks have been recently found, while digging trenches for water pipe lines. An image of Kartikeya was also recovered from the ruins. This shows that there was a Saivite temple at the site and it was probably contemporaneous with the ruined temple of Doul Govinda. Near Doul Govinda on the hill, rocks were partially blown off and must have been carried for chisellisation of sculptures and architectural remains. Just on the bank of the Brahmaputa at Manikarneswar, on the top of a hillock, there is a modern temple. But the site yields the ruins of a pre Ahom temple, consisting of broken *Dwarsakhas, Amalakas* etc. Evidently there must have been a temple in the pre Ahom age. Old chiseled stone blocks can be seen at the residences of the local people in the locality.

To the north of Manikarneswar temple at a distance of about 3 km there is a temple on the hill, built in the days of the Ahoms. The name of the temple is Dirgheswari. The site has a few fragments of architectural pieces of an old temple. A few rock cut miniature pre Ahom *sikhara* designs are noticed here.

The pilgrimage

As a devotee proceeds to the Doul Govinda temple he or she feels elated by the beauty of the surroundings passes by on the way. The journey is more pleasant and attractive if made by crossing the river by steamer service from the south bank. As the steamer, it may be also an engined boat, leaves the south bank at Guwahati the pilgrim leaves behind him the temples of Sukreswara Shiva and Janardan at the river side and passes by the small rocky islets of *Karmanasha* and *Urvashi* and the Shiva shrine on the rock Umananda midstream mythologically known as *Bhasmachala* where a crowded Shivratri *mela* is a big attraction every year. The steamer or the engined boat moves north eastern direction towards the green hillock of Manikarneswar at the north bank where the temple of Mani Shila Maheswar, another shrine of attraction for devotees of Lord Shiva, specially on the Shivratri day is located about five kilometers downstream to the west is sighted the Saraighat Bridge, a bridge constructed over the Brahmaputra on the wake of 1962 Chinese aggression. Nearer in the north west comes up the view of the hillock of Ashwaklanta. In summer, the sandy alluvious midstream as well as on the banks of the river get submerged under water to come up again in winter, but the green all around interspersed with full bloom red flowers of *Krishna Chura* groves gives soothing to eyes. During this time the current sweeping in the river with whirlpools here and there and the steamer or engined boat takes longer almost half an hour or sometimes more, moving upstream to reach the north bank. But the return journey takes only half the time to reach the south bank. In winter the trip takes only a few minutes to cross the river which is reduced to only half a kilometer in its span, with sluggish current midstream.

The temple premises of Lord Doul Govinda is only a few minutes walk from the ferry approach at the river bank. The pilgrim walks down .the actual Rajaduar.

Pilgrims who travel by road crossing the river over the Saraighat bridge through the other side in the west, hillocks all around leaving behind the Nilachal Bhubaneswari hills with temples of Mother Goddess Kamakhya and Goddess Bagala Devi and Bhubaneswari thereon. They get only distant view of the sights to the east, that experienced by one who crosses the river by steamer or boat. It is about half an hour journey by vehicle from Saraighat Bridge to the temple of Doul Govinda.

The Sacred Performances

The sacred geography that has been discussed earlier is the one of the few instances of the intangible heritages of the ethnic Assamese people. These intangible heritages initiates in the sacred centers in the form of ritualistic practices derived from the great tradition either through text or from the collective memory.

Daily prayer services

Different types of congregational services are included in the daily prayer routine of the temple. These services continue from morning till the early hours of evening. The singing of hymns and songs, the chanting of prayers to the accompaniment of musical instruments and the reading and explaining of Bhagawat Gita, constitute the chief features of the services. Besides, following the rules prescribed in vedic literature *puja*, *bhog*, *arati* and *sayan* of the Lord is preformed here.

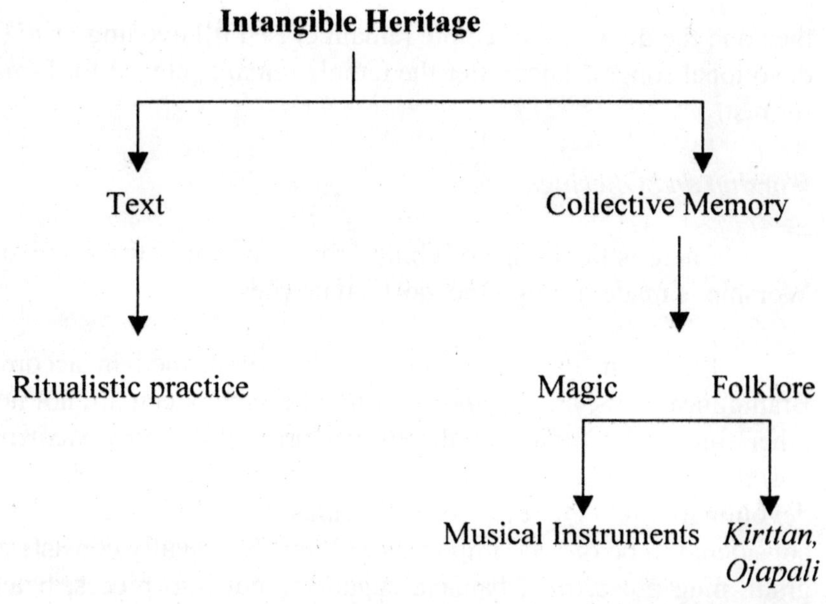

Every morning the doors of the Lords temple are opened by about 6.30am. *Archana* (worshipping rituals) is performed by the priests after giving bath to the Lord. Everyday the Lord is given bath with fresh water mixed with milk, *tulsi*, *chandan*, *karpur*, *agaru* and flowers and then dressed up with new cloths. Devotees start gathering in the mandir premise by about 8 O'clock. They all stand in queue for their turn to pay their tributes. Before that, they light the earthen lamp locally called '*chaki*' and incense sticks on an altar specially allotted for the purpose. After offering prayer and getting blessings as chanted by the priests receiving *nirmali* and *pad jal* (transcendent offerings), devotees seat in rows in the open hall. At noon, the priest offer the Lord *Bhoga* (rice boiled in milk with sugar) and closes the main door of the temple. He then bows down just outside the door, *daba* (a big conical drum) is beaten accompanied by bell and blowing of Conch, all the devotees bow down along with. After that, the volunteers of the temple management start distributing *prasada* followed by *bhoga* among the devotees which the devotees take with great reverence to Lord Doul Govinda. Most of the devotees contribute to the temple and offer milk and others as *prasada*. Such devotees get some amount of *prasada* as their share from the counter. The devotees dispersed then and the door of the temple remain closed till evening *arati* (singing of devotional songs). Thereafter the temple remains closed for Lord's retiring for rest.

Worship and Offerings

There is the image of child Krishna which is worshipped everyday. Worship is made through the vaishnavite rites.

Except in case of image worship performed in accordance with Brahminical rites, all the *upacaras* numbering sixteen are not necessary in other forms of worship or devotional practices. *Pancopacaras* (*gandha*, *puspa*, *deepa* and *naivedya*) are sufficient enough for an ordinary devotional rite. Of the five upacaras, the offering of *naivedya* is considered to be of vital importance. *Naivedya* usually consists of softened gram, mug pulse, rice, banana, sugarcane cut into pieces, betel nuts and other palatable things that could be offered uncooked. The softened or germinated gram (*gaji*) and pulses mixed with rice are considered the main elements of *naivedya*. Others are mere accessories.

Things offered to the deity are having some symbolic significance. It is believed, devotees ignorant of those symbolic significance, do not get the full merit for partaking of the offerings. This assignment of symbolical meaning is called *tattva-vicara*. To quote a few, the canopy hung over the image stands for hood of the mythological serpent *Sesa* (*Ananta*) and the light that burns before the image stands for knowledge. The plantain leaves used for distributing offerings symbolize *Bhakti* and *naivedya* signifies the grace of God. In this way everything used or offered to the deity in a devotional ceremony has been linked up or associated with the vaishnava cult.

Sacred observances

The following types of observances in Doul Govinda temple have been described in the succeeding pages: (i) festival (ii) ceremonies connected with death anniversaries of saints (iii) special devotional functions.

Festivals

Festivals of the Vaishnava sects observed in Doul Govinda are mainly related to some incidents or episodes of Krishna's life and are mostly identical with those of other parts of India. In addition to those three bihus, the traditional festival of the Brahmaputra valley is also observed with appropriate manner. Following are some of the main festivals observed-

Maghi Purnima

One of the auspicious day is the full moon night of the month of *Magha* (*Maghi Purnima*) which in some years comes off in the month of Fagun also. Several thousands of devotees gather on this day turning the mandir campus a sea of people. Despite the number, devotees conduct themselves with discipline until late hours in the afternoon. *Bhoga* is cooked in quintals on this sacred day for the devotees of whom many pool their mite for the purpose, the devotees come here to pray to Lord Doul Govinda for fulfillment of their desire.

Phalgutsava

The festival of Holi is celebrated with great pomp and joy. Spring brings new life to nature and the surroundings gets festive mood. This liveliness is reflected in the festival of Holi. This is the festival of fun making, it is a festival of colour throwing at each other. Shri Krishna is brought into a mythology to show that Lord himself made fun with his women friends – the *Gopis* going to the houses of his another spouse Ghunusha Devi to live with the period lingering to five days which fact enraged Lord's consort Goddess Laxmi and she engages her devotees to put a barricade on Lord's way back home.

This festival is celebrated with well programmed rituals and merry making in the campus of Shri Shri Doul Govinda temple at Rajaduar. The agenda begins with the *Meish Dah* ritual on the previous evening of the full moon night of the month of *Falguna*, occasionally the month of *Chaitra*. The *Mesh Dah* ritual is symbolical burning of sheep inside an improvised temporary shed of hey. The image of lord Doul Govinda is then taken out of the sanctum and placed on a throne inside the Doul which is a separate altar at a little distance. Lord's image is kept there for five days during which period, large number of devotees come to offer, *abir* or *Faku* powder specially made for the occasion. This is not exactly vermilion, but looks like that, but a bit pinkish . The routine *Puja Archana* combined with *Homa–Yagya* are performed at the Doul on these days. The campus becomes a place of merry –making with singing devotional songs, *Nam-Kirtan*, *Oza pali* performance. All the nights are kept allotted for *Bhawana*, a classical form of Assamese Dance –drama performance and such parties are invited from outside also on these days besides the Local groups . On the last days of the festival, Lord Doul Govinda is taken out for *Parikrama* (going round) symbolizing return from the house of Devi (Ghunusha) .The procession is a grand one with band party beating of *Dhols* and *Khols* (local drums) and groups singing Holi-songs dancing with *Faku* powder smeared all over the body and clothes and throwing of such powder to the sky. Residents of both sex, young, old and children – join the procession. People offer obeisance to Lord Doul Govinda kneeling down and bowing head placing a *Sarai* with *Gamocha* on a piece of plantain leave and lighting earthen lamp when the procession passes by the frontage of their houses. The procession proceeds westward to the place of the Dehing Satra about 5 kilometers away from the temple premises and return there from after being received with due reverence, when the procession comes back to the temple Campus, a barricade is put blocking the Lord's way into the sanctum symbolizing (*Ghunusa Jatra*) the enragement of Goddess Laxmi . But the barricade is overpowered by the Lords devotees and Lord Doul Govinda is placed on the throne at the sanctum sanctorum.

Janmastami

Shri Krishna *Janmastami* is celebrated with great reverence in the month of *Bhadra* in the premises. This annual celebration draws a large number of devotees. Local residents remain awake almost the whole night to attend the *puja* and *home yagya*, singing devotional songs in praise of Lord Vishnu.

Bihu

The three *Bihus* observed in the last day of *Asvina, Pausa* and *Chaitra* are respectively known as *Kati Bihu*, *Magh Bihu* and *Bahag Bihu.*

On *Kati Bihu*, the Lord Shalegram is worshipped here, besides the other observances like plantation of basil plant (*tulsi*) and offering of light (*dipadana*) to the plant etc. This act of offering light continues throughout the month.

The *Magh Bihu*, is celebrated with bone-fires and feasts. Villagers gather in the temple campus and bone-fire (*Meji*) is observed with congregational prayers and music. Food prepared from newly harvested crop is offered to the deity.

Bohag-Bihu is observed in the villages for three to seven days with special devotional programme. On the first day of the *Baishakh* month, i.e. the New Years Day according to Indian calendar, villagers take holy dip in the river Brahmaputra and come straight to the temple and worship the Lord and *Nam-prasanga* (singing of devotional songs) is arranged. It is indeed a much waited occasion to start a new year.

Ceremonies

Death anniversary of Sankardeva and Madhavdeva are observed with due solemnity. Birthday of Sankardeva is also celebrated with great pomp and joy.

Special devotional functions

There are a few more devotional functions that do not come within the above mentioned categories. One of such celebration is the foundation day of the temple. The day comes on the *Akshay Tritiya tithi* of *Baishakh* month (mid April-mid May). The villagers take active part in this celebration. Plantein tree is placed at the entrance of the temple and all the religious rites like recitation of Bhagawat, singing of devotional songs etc. takes place.

There is a annual calendar which could be related to Annual Agricultural cycle of the people around the sacred geography that is north Guwahati in this case. There are significant cultural practices of this territory and they could be identified as 'local identity'. The Doul Govinda being the structural center point creates there network of sacred performances for the last five hundred years or so resulting in a representative of intangible heritages.

The Sacred Specialists

The study of the sacred specialists is important in the context of eco museum parameters due to the fact that the sacred specialists are the interpreter of the culture as well as the carrier of the human heritages within the sacred geography. A number of specialists are intimately responsible for collective memory resulting in survival of the intangible heritages in the territory. When we talk about the sacred specialists and other people, one aspect is to be noted here that all the people including the sacred specialists associate themselves with the Doul Govinda voluntarily and there is a democratic understanding in this act which is significant for an eco museum set up.

There are numbers of persons assigned with different functions of the Doul Govinda temple. They are the persons who cultivate, preserve and promote the temple as a sacred.

At present for the efficient management of the temple and for conducting the religious services regularly, there are two categories of functionaries. The first category is the management committee with around 25 members who do not take part in religious activities but in charge of the management of the temple. The other category is known as *Pujari* (Priests) who conduct religious rites.

The temple is managed by a committee of twenty-five members constituted by General Assembly for a period of three years. There are two Secretaries, one for administration and another for financial responsibility. Both the Secretaries are the executive head and their duty is of various nature. They are to look after all the matters relating to the day-to-day affairs of the temple. The executive committee plans out all the development programmes and the members execute them. The works can be executed only with the approval of the executive committee. The committee has so far taken up several such development works, specially for the comfort and convenience of the pilgrims and visitors who visit the temple daily from different parts of Assam. With the grant of Rs. 16 Lac received from present Prime Minister of India Dr. Manmohan Singh, who was then MP, Rajyasabha, the committee has constructed a pilgrims guest house adjacent to the temple. Likewise with the grant received from a local Member of Legislative Assembly, a rest shade had been built in the temple premises.

The second categories of functionaries who take part in religious activities are again in charge of different departments. This group of functionaries is not only involved with worship but also with all sorts of religious arrangements. The practice of worship of the image of Lord Govinda forms an indispensable part of the daily devotional routine. The man who is placed in charge of worshipping image is known as *Pujari*. Under him one or more assistance whose duties are to prepare sandal paste, arrange *naivedya*, to supply with garlands and flowers etc. In other words, they are in the management of the *manikut*, i.e. the sanctum sanctorium.

From morning till the evening hours a series of sacred functions are held in the temple. Here so many villagers are also involved. They neither reside in the temple premise nor the member of the committee, but they arrange congregational prayer services. There are orchestral parties also, known as *gayan-bayan*. The leader of the vocal musicians is called *Gayan*. These parties are also formed with the villagers. Lastly there are *Natuwas*, skilled in the art of dancing, *Dhuliyas* (drum players) and *Khuliyas* (flute players), whose duty is to entertain the deity as well as the devotees who assemble in the temple on different occasions.

There are a few more functionaries who are not directly connected with any of the above departments but work for the general management of the institution. The Secretary who is in charge of the finance department is the treasurer. He is the custodian of valuable properties. He keeps accounts of the income derived from devotees. He is also required to keep regular accounts of expenditure incurred in connection with the management of the temple. He however has got subordinates to assist him in the work. There is a store department of the temple. There are functionaries who are engaged in this department. They have to look after the offerings of the devotees.

In above the types of sacred specialists and their functions has been discussed. Besides the hierchy or the responsibilities of the specialists, another important thing to strike the notice that, there are many villagers of different age groups who work as **volunteer** in the temple. All villagers, irrespective of caste and creed are welcome in the temple. Therefore one can observe old man of the villages, sometimes even students also distributing *Prasad* to the devotees in the afternoon. Some keeps vigil and assist the devotees.

Cultural Mapping

Cultural mapping is a process that facilitates identification of a given territory and their human heritage. These assets are of varied nature and are the parts of the complex whole in which both the tangible and intangible elements exists. For example, music (sounds), dance (movements), icons (symbols),crafts (artifacts), language(expression), spiritual (mystical), geographic(totemic), botanical(environmental) etc. The significance of cultural mapping lies in the fact that it serves as data bank. It is the method through which one can systematically document cultural centers, heritage sites, cultural elements, arts, crafts, customs and traditions of a region or territory. Cultural mapping hence is significant in the context of eco museum parameters. The outcomes of the cultural mapping help a community to identify their cultural assets which are the identity of the people of a particular territory. UNESCO defines 'cultural identity' as the correspondence between a community (national, ethnic, linguistic etc.) and its cultural life as the right of each community to its own culture. In other words, cultural mapping of an ecomuseum territory helps the community to conserve living cultural elements reflecting the local identity.

Cultural mapping of the Doul Govinda sacred complex have been made in order to establish the local identity of the people of the entire *kshetra* or the territory. Both the tangible and the intangible in situ elements have been incorporated in this cultural mapping. The study of the historical significance of the area will reflect the cultural character of the territory. The Doul Govinda *kshetra* has been inhabited by Assamese people. The word Assamese is a broad term, which includes a multiethnic people. Both tribal and non tribal people have together formed the Assamese society. But each group of people have their own tradition and they are maintaining them even remaining within the broad framework. This typical Assamese identity is reflected in the way of life, manners, habits, material culture, arts and crafts, religious practices, various tangible and intangible heritage of the territory. In other words, by cultural mapping attempt has been made to recognize the integrated heritage of the people of the Doul Govinda sacred complex.

Cultural Landscape

Doul Govinda sacred complex is located in north Guwahati of Kamrup district of Assam. It is the gateway to the greater Indian culture, i.e. gateway of Gangetic plains on the west and also to south east Asia. In such a multicultural milieu it is important to understand the characteristics of the territory.

The Physical Background of the Territory

Assam is the frontier province of India on the north east. The boundaries of Assam lie between latitudes 28°18' and 24° north and longitudes 89°46' and 97°4' east. It contains at present an area of 54,000 square miles of which a little over 24,000 square miles constitute the plains districts, 19,500 the southern hill tracts and the rest the trail hill tracts to the north. The Brahmaputra valley of assam is surrounded on all sides by the mountain and hill ranges like a fort. In the north the eastern Himalayan range which continues towards south east and give rise to the sub Himalayan range of Patkai. The Patkai ranges have link with the north Cachar hills, hills of Karbi Anglong and continues with the Khasi and Garo hills of the south west. Though the heart of the province runs the great river called in Sanskrit the Brahmaputra or Shri Lauhitya. In Assamese it is called *Lohit* or *Luit*. It enters the north eastern corner of Assam through the Mishmi hills and turning nearly due west, passes through all the districts of Assam. It is the chief artery of Assam.[1] For generations the people of Assam have intimate relationship with the Brahmaputra both the sacred and secular – their whole history and culture have emanated from the Brahmaputra river. Assam has always held a distinct and independent political existence, though her political frontiers have advanced or receded according to her prosperity and at times her area varied greatly from what it is today. It must however be noted that although the political boundaries of the country have changed from age to age, its geographical limits have been marked out by nature in such a manner as to ensure that it retained its cultural identity through ages. The unbroken unity of its history and culture is the result of the geographical unity of the area of the Brahmaputra valley. This is a kind of diversity within the homogenous super structure – cultural distinctiveness as noticed in north south and east west direction.

Brahmaputra valley is a compact geographical unit comprising several districts and one of the major districts being the Kamrup.

The Literary and Folkloristic Significance

The Pragjyotispura was referred in great epics like Mahabharata. There are references of Pragjyotispura as a famous kingdom in Mahabharata. It was known to be a kingdom ruled by Bhagadatta and in some passages kingdom ruled over by the demons Naraka and Muru. Ramayana ascribes the founding of the kingdom of Pragjyotisa to Amurtarajas, one of the four sons of a great king Kusa. Again Markandeya Purana says, Amurtarajas as the name is generally written in the Mahabharata is mentioned there simply as father of the famous king Gaya. It places Pragjyotisa on the face of the tortoise[1]. It is also mentioned in the list of the peoples of the east as given by Varahamihira in the Brihat Samhita. The same statement is found in the Matsya and Brahmanda Puranas (Barua, 2003:11). The Bhagawat Purana refers to Pragjyotisa when recounting the story of Naraka.

The kalika Puran, a work of the 10th century AD says, formerly Brahma staying here created the stars, so the city is called Pragjyotisapura, a city equal to the city of Indra. This etymological explanation given by the kalika Puran has been followed by the historians of Assam. Gait writes, '*Prag* means former or eastern and *Jyotisa* a star, astrology, shining. Pragjyotishpur, may, therefore, be taken to mean the city of eastern astrology. The name is in connection with the reputation which the country has always held as a land of magic and witchcrafts. It was in Assam that the *Tantrik* form of Hinduism originated (Gait, 2001:15) Historian Kanaklal Barua accepts the etymology but explains in a different connotation. It is significant that to the immediate east of the town of

1 Chapter 58 of Kurmavibhaga, describes Pragjyotisha on the face of the tortoise.

Guwahati there is a temple on the crest of a hill known as *Citrascala* and this temple is dedicated to the *Navagrahas* or nine planets. It is probable that this temple could be related to the name Pragjyotisapura. There is another version that Pragjyotisa seems to be connected with topographical features of the land rather than with any religious cult. References illustrate that *Pragjyotisa* or Pragjyotisapura was on an extensive hill. Thus, Pragjyotisa may be a sanskrtization of a non Aryan formation.

It has been described in the kalika Purana that immediately after Naraka of Mithila became king and was placed in charge of the Goddess Kamakhya, the name of the land was changed from Pragjyotisa to Kamarupa. The term *Kamarupa* (Kamakhya) symbolized a new cult, and in exaltation of the land itself was rechristened. The earliest epigraphic reference to Kamarupa is however to be found in the well-known Allahabad inscription of Samudragupta where Kamarupa is mentioned as a frontier territory. In classical Sanskrit literature Pragjyotisa and Kamarupa occur side by side, for instance, in Kalidasa. In the story of Raghu's *digvijaya* as given in the *Raghuvamsa* the hero first came to Pragjyotisa and then to Kamarupa after having crossed the *Lauhitya*. The king of Kamarupa worshipped Raghu's feet on a golden foot –stool as if they were his presiding deity with presents of jewels instead of flowers. Yadavaprakasa (c. 1000 A.D) in his Vaijayanti also mentions Pragjyotisa and Kamarupa: *Pragjyotisa Kamarupa pragjalika*. Rajasekhara (c. 900 A.D) refers to Pragjyotisa as a country and Kamarupa as a mountain. The Jaina lexicographer Hemacandra (c. 1200 A.D) says. "the Pragjyotisas are the Kamarupas". Purusottama also states that Pragjyotisa is Kamarupa, Yasodhara (c. 1300 A.D) the authors of the Jayamangala commentary on the *Kamasutra*, places kamrupa as a country of the eastern region. The Manjusri Mulakalpa puts it near the Himalayas. There are lots of confusion in the text about the exact position of the territory whether it is Pragjyotispura or Kamrupa.

In some of the later Puranas the name appears in a different context. The Siva Purana states that in *Sahyadri*, there was a country named kamrupa which was conquered by a *Raksas* named Bhima. Both Vayu and Brahmanda Puranas referring to the peaks of that mountain

Devakuta and their dwellers mention the *Kamrupi Raksasa*. From these texts it is apparent that in ancient time this territory was the seat of witch crafts or magic and people have supernatural power.

A fairly detailed account of the topography of the country is to be found in the Kalika Purana and the Yogini Tantra (C.1600 AD), both the works being devoted to the religious history of medieval Assam. The Kalika Purana says that Kamrupa lies to the east of the Karotaya river[2]. According to the Yogini Tantra the country lying to the east of Karotaya as far as Dikkaravasini is called Kamrupa. It is triangular in shape (*trikonakaram*) and a hundred *yojanas* in length, spreading over an area of thirty *yojanas*. The Visnu Purana also stated that the country extended around the temple of Kamrupa (which was in the center of Kamrupa) in all directions for 100 *yojanas*. Thus Kamrupa included roughly the Brahmaputra valley, Bhutan, Rangpur and Cooch Bihar (Barua, 2003: 14-15).

A later Sanskrit work called Haragaurisamvada divides Kamrupa into four *pithas* with clearly marked river boundaries, viz, (i) *Ratnapitha*, between the *Karotaya* and *Swarnakosa* (ii) *Kamapitha*, between the *Swarnakosa* and the *Kapili* (iii) *Swarnapitha*, between the *Puspika* and the *Bhairavi* (iv) *Saumara*, between the *Bhairavi* and *Dikrang* river.

According to the Chinese pilgrim Hiuen Tsiang who visited the court of Bhaskaravarman in 643 AD, the country was more than 1667 miles in circuit. The pilgrim traveled from Pundravardhana on the east more than 150 miles, crossed a large river and reached Kamrupa. The pilgrim says that to the east of Kamrupa was a series of hills and hillocks without any principal city stretching to southwestern China. The name Kamrupa according to the Puranic legends is associated with Kamdeva, the God of love. It is here that Kama was sent by the Gods to put an end to

---

2 *The Karotaya was once a large and sacred river which was known to have flowed through the northern part of modern Bengal and is referred to in the Tirthayatra section of the Vanaparva of the Mahabharata. It is also said that at the wedding of Shiva and Parvati, the water poured upon their hands, fell to the ground and became the river Karotaya, from kara, the hand and toya the water.*

Shiva's mourning after the death of his consort and to awaken in him again the passion of creation. He was burnt to ashes by the angry glance of the great God, but later recovered his original form (*rupa*), hence the name Kamrupa. During the medieval period Kamrupa became a centre of tantrik worship and considered as a most sacred place, specially the temple of Kamakhya where the Devi was adored.

This worship of the Goddess and the very names of Kamakhya and Kamrupa seem to lead the notion that the cult was probably derived from some Pre Aryan concept. There may be further connection of Kamrupa with such Austric formations as *Kamru* or *Kamrut* which in Santhali is a name for a lesser divinity. The term *Kamaru* or *kamru* as alternative form of Kamrupa is attested in the Buddhist Caryas and also in Haragaurismavada.

Archaeological Significance

Assam has its cultural roots since prehistoric period. It has passed through late stone age and neolothic age, however does not witness the Bronze Age civilization as compared to the Indus Valley civilization. There is no witness of rock cuts or cave paintings as well. The art of stone sculpture in Assam is not earlier than 1st century AD. At Guwahati and its neighbourhood curved images have been found in abundance. The huge Vishnu at Ashwaklanta on the north bank of the Brahmaputra depict the mastery skill of the sculptor. Besides, the findings of Amabri excavation the sand stone Nataraja Shiva, the Nrittyarata Ganpati, the black stone images of Vishnu, Brahma, Indra of the 10th-11th cent AD, the metal images of Vishnu and Durga, now preserved in Assam State Museum are few examples of fine specimens of iconoplastic art so far unearthed.

At the Nilachal hill, near Kamakhya temple, a well known *Shakti* temple, a good number of stone sculptures dating from 8th – 17th cent AD have been found. A few of them have been preserved at the site under the provisions of the Ancient Monument Preservation Act. A special reference may be made to the stone gateway that dates back to the period of Naranarayana, the famous Koch king of the 16th cent. AD who rebuild the temple of Mother Goddess Kamakhya. The gateway has a pointed arch and decorated in relief work with lotus medallions and *vyala* lions on either side of the gate.

The Kamrupa was quite close to Magadha, where Budhhist influences reigned supreme. It is surprising that ancient Kamrupa was less effected by such influences, yet it was like a paradox (Dutt, 1959: 21). Yuan Chang said that in the 7th century the people of Kamrupa worshipped the *'Devas'* and had no faith in Buddhism and hence from the time when Buddha appeared in the world to 7th Cent. there had not yet been built one *Sangharama* as a place for priests to assemble. Briefly speaking, there were a few Buddhist in ancient Kamrupa who were respected by the king and Buddhism did actually exist in the country but did not flourish to a widely extent. This is evident and born out by this fact that there are only a few specimens of Buddhist sculpture so far discovered in Assam.

Plastic art in Assam degenerated to a considerable extent during the Ahom period that ranges from 13th cent till the advent of the British rule. It is evident that art lacked royal support and sympathy until the Ahom rulers converted themselves to Hinduism. Ahoms were mostly busy in political activities and rarely payed any attention to art and craft. The stone sculptures from Ambari in Guwahati such as the four armed image of Surya and the two armed image of Vishnu reveal the classical tradition that survived in isolated pockets during Ahom era. The majority of the stone sculptures discovered in the Ambari excavation in the heart of the Guwahati city are now preserved in Assam State Museum and they bear the characteristics of the pre Ahom i.e. the Pala art style of Assam. The famous Ambari Nataraja, a splendid work of art also bear some degenerated elements in its pre Ahom style. However, the terracotta sculptures discovered from this site show sophistication in style. It is to be noticed that the stone carvers of 10th – 12th cent were followed by the metal and clay work. Like stone art, the metal and terracotta art in Assam reached its zenith by 12th cent AD. The figures became cylindrical and stele became decorative. The terracotta of 11th – 12th cent from Assam bear classical style and form (Chaudhury, 2000:3). The metal image of Indra from Kahilipara, Guwahati preserved in the Assam State Museum and three terracotta plaques showing the figures of Bhringi, a dancing figure and an aristocratic lady are few examples of sophisticated art.

17th cent. witness the revival of stone art in Assam only when Ahom kings wanted to build or rebuild Hindu temples that were destroyed due to earthquake or other natural calamities. The walls of the temple were decorated with sculptured images. Some of the images appeared to be recovered from the debris of the earlier temples. Hence, although these temples belong to the times of Ahom and Koch rulers, all the images were not contemporary with the newly built temples on the old temple sites, quite a few of them were of pre Ahom period. The Ahom artists were again perhaps not well versed in the classical Sanskrit tradition of pre Ahom,i.e, Palas, hence these works of art are found highly impregnated with folk elements. They were not well versed with Hindu iconography, so mistakes were committed while portraying the figures of Hindu deity. For e.g the image of Vishnu in seated posture found in Janardan temple of Sukreswar. The image reflects the unsuccessful attempt of the carves of imitating the Pala figures.

The history of metal, bronze and brass images are later than the stones. The earliest image is dated to 9th to 10th cent.AD. These images also display the characteristics of Pala period. The images are found sometimes in hoards buried at different places of Brahmaputra valley. One of such hoards were located at Narakasur or Kahilipara of southern part of present Guwahati city. The objects are now preserved in Assam State Museum. One of the important art objects of this hoard is the image of Indra, which is considered as one of the excellent art work of the period. Another significant piece of work is *Devi* (*Mahisasurmardini*) depicted in a round medallion. These works are dated to 10th – 12th cent.

The images that appeared in wood also covers a wide area of sculptural heritage of Assam. These images have decayed with the passage of time, as the heavy rain and humid climatic condition of Assam is not suitable for their better preservation. Few such remains are however found in various satras of Assam.

The clay was another medium in which works of art were produced. They were either hand modeled or casted. The ancient most clay work found in Assam has been dated back to 6th cent. AD. Such burn clay or terracotta images of 10th – 12th cent. have been found in old sites of Guwahati. Recently some terracotta plaques have been discovered from the Cotton College, Guwahati campus and they show similarity in style with the remains already preserved in Assam State Museum. All of them are the products of indigenous style, which allowed sophistication to some extent. These all are in high relief and display pre Ahom styles. Mention should also be made here of the brick temples at Kamakhya decorated with clay sculptures. These are now in the verge of extinction.

North Guwahati was important place during the days of Narakasura and Bhagadatta, who was killed in the famous battle of Mahabharata. North Guwahati as the Kamrupa Nagar was the capital of Dharampala, one of the ruler of Pala dynasty. The Koch king Parikshit Narayan established his capital here and was named as '*Durjay Nagar*'. The '*Parikshit pukhuri*' and '*Konwari Pukhuri*' at Shilsako of north Guwahati tell the old tales of Koch dynasty. The Ahoms took over from the Koch rulers in 1625 AD occupied the city and since then north Guwahati received care and patronage for its growth. The rulers confined their strategic installations within the south bank and shifted the administrative outpost to Rajaduar on the north bank. Since those days north Guwahati has been serving as the imperial gateway for further expansion of Ahom kingdom. Obviously north Guwahati attained the status of an administrative seat which promoted residential and other associated activities. North Guwahati was made administrative seat for its natural fortifications which still prevails.

The name north Guwahati has been used during the reign of Ahom kings when Barphukan and Paniphukan, the two royal Generals ruled over it. Till the advent of Britishers, north Guwahati was more important than the southern part. When the British established the capital of Assam in Shillong (present capital of Meghalaya), the importance gradually shifted to southern part leaving north Guwahati with the old historical and mythological ruins.

For war strategy, north Guwahati was the best place and has been proved on many occasions. In the past every battle fought here was won. The famous battle of Saraighat was fought here in north Guwahati under the leadership of Lachit Barphukan with the Mughal army lead by Ram Singh besides Syed Chena and Sayed Firoz, the two Generals were defeated by Assamese soldiers here. Bokhtiar Khilizi was also defeated here. The famous stone inscription-'kanai barashi boa' describe all these facts in old Assamese script. Rudra Singh, the Ahom king encamped here with a large army to invade north Bengal but unfortunately he died of severe attack of small pox and the whole mission was defeated.

Historian Kanaklal Barua (Barua, 1992: 14) assumes that the capital named 'Kamrup Nagar', the city of Kamrud of the Muslim chroniclers, was at north Guwahati near the temple of Aswaklanta. The *Kamrupar Buranji* mentions the tradition that a king named Dharampala had his seat of government there. The modern town of north Guwahati possesses temples, roads, bridges, fortifications and moats which are clearly pre Ahom origin. There are two temples on the Aswaklanta hill. The upper temple contains the image of Vishnu lying on Ananta Sajya. As mentioned above it is one of the finest specimens of sculptural skill in Kamrupa in the beginning of 12th century. The western part of the town is called Shilsako, because it still contains a small stone built bridge over a stream. The eastern part is known as Rajaduar (king's gate), which shows that a palace was there. The second copper plate of Dharampala was actually found in the village of Rangmahal about two miles to the north of Rajaduar. This is another indication that the capital was then at north Guwahati.

In above the archaeological significance of the territory of north Guwahati as well as Kamrup district has been discussed. Here to be noted that archaeological significance of modern Kamrup district has only been taken into account. If we consider the ancient Kamrup, almost whole of present Assam and also part of modern Bengal will come under coverage. Therefore present study has been limited to present day Kamrup district where the territory of the proposed eco museum is located. The significance have been studied because they are associated with the collective memory of the people of the territory which are very important in reference to eco museum. The representation of the tangible aspect of these memories are now preserved in the Assam State Museum, Guwahati.

It will be important here to discuss the role of the Assam state Museum. This particular museum serves as the representation of the tangible heritage of the territory. The Assam State Museum was established by the Kamrup Anusandhan Samiti in 1940 and was a non government establishment in its initial stage. In 1953, it was taken over by the state government. The collection of the museum have been displayed as well as stored in different sections such as the epigraphy section (which includes various rock inscriptions of historic periods of Assam), sculpture section, natural history section, arts and crafts section, textile section, musical instrument section, literature section where photographs and paintings of eminent personalities of Assam have been displayed, ethnographic section representing the material culture of various ethnic groups of north east India, arms and weapons section and in the newly extended part of the building a village life gallery and tribal life style have been displayed.

Thus for the tangible representation of the heritage of the proposed territory there is the Assam State Museum, but for the intangible heritage of this territory, a model to be reconstructed. For understanding of historical and cultural significance of the tangible heritages it is necessary to link them spiritually and emotionally. There seems to be a possibility to develop a heritage trail in this case.

Heritage Trail

The heritage trail planned within the Doul Govinda eco museum territory would engulf heritage sites on the both bank of the river Brahmaputra. In this heritage outline the historicity of site as well as its folkloristic significance would be taken as the criteria to mark the circuit.

The central point of this trail will be the Assam State Museum. For the convenient of the visitor the trail has been constructed in uni-directional order. Below the heritage centres has been spotted in the map and the significance of each centre has been discussed one by one.

Vasisthashram

This sacred centre is situated in the southern-most rim of Guwahati city on the Sandhyachal hill. It is called *Vasisthashram*, after the great vedic Sage Vashistha, who is said to have lived here amidst a beautiful natural surroundings. Three rivulets named *Sandhya*, *Lalita* and *Kanta* meet here and flow perennially adding scenic grandeur to the place. A ritual bath here is said to increase longevity. A temple of Siva is also attached to the hermitage of Vasistha. During *Shivratri* a large number of devotees gather here to offer their worship. This is also an ideal picnic spot for the picnickers. The devotees visit *Vasisthashrama* and take bath in the stream nearby to wash off their sins. The present temple in *Vasisthashrama*, which is incidentally the last Ahom monument in the neighbourhood of Guwahati, was built in the second half of the 18th century by King Rajesvar Singh of the Ahom dynasty.

There are many legends about sage Vasistha. There is also a legend that connects Vasistha with the origin of the Ahom kings. It is said that, Vasistha used to do his *'sandhya arati'* (evening prayer) in a stream near his hermitage. One day, God Indra with his queen Shachi and other heavenly women came down from heaven and began playing in the same stream. As a result of this amorous sport the water of the stream became impure. Seeing all this sage Vasistha grew furious and cursed Indra, saying that he would have sexual intercourse with a Daitya woman. Indra was at once transformed into a normal man and had sexual intercourse with a woman. He, however, granted a boon to that woman saying that the son in her womb would become a king. He was the progenitor of the Ahom dynasty. According to some legends Vasistha was initiated into the secrets of the *Sakta* practices and got spiritual success. It is probable that Vasistha came down at *Sandhya Kal* (evening), after he was not allowed to enter the Kamakhya temple and meditated on Shiva.

Srimanta Sankardeva Kalakshetra

It has been set up as a grand exposition of the life and culture of the people of Assam. This Kalakshetra is named after Srimanta Sankaradeva, the greatest Vaishnava saint and the greatest integrator of the Assamese society. The Kalakshetra is a multi Arts complex. It houses a museum where the material culture of different ethnic groups are preserved and exhibited, an open air theatre with a capacity of 2000 audience to hold folk festival, dance and drama, an artists village where one can experience the atmosphere of the village life of Assam, Sahitya Bhawan which is a library of rare books and manuscripts, the Lalit Kala Bhawan which has sufficient space for holding exhibitions or workshops and a heritage park.

Navagraha Temple

Navagraha temple or the temple of nine planets is one of the major centre for astronomical and astrological studies. Nestled in Chitrachal Hill of south eastern part of Guwahati, Navagraha temple bears the proof of astronomical practice in Assam for hundreds of years. Here Navagrahas or nine celestial bodies are represented by nine 'Shivalingas' each covered with a coloured garment, symbolic of each of the celestial bodies. The nine planetary Gods,viz. *surya* (Sun), *Chandra* (Moon), *Mangala* (Mars), *Budha* (Mercury), *Brihaspati* (Jupiter), *Sukra* (Venus), *Sani* (Saturn), *Rahu* and *Ketu* are worshipped inside the main temple. There is not much historical evidence on Navagraha temple. But this is fact that Assam has always remained a great centre of study of astronomy and astrology and therefore Assam is referred as Pragjyotishpur in may ancient literature.

Navagraha temple was built during the reign of Ahom King Rajeswar Singha in the late 17th cent. This is traceable from the inscription on the temple walls. However some historians opines that the stone structure of the temple dates back to 11th cent and only the brick structure is of Ahom period. The stone blocks inside the temple belong to the Pala period of 10th – 11th cent. where the ancient astronomical studies were performed.

Sukreswara

The temple is located on the southern bank of the river Brahmaputra in Assam. The hillock in which the temple located is called *Hasti* (as in the the Kalika Purana) and described as the *ashrama* (hermitage) of the sage Sukra. The temple was built by King Pramatta Singh of the Ahom dynasty in 1744 A.D. According to the Kalika Purana, *Sukreswara Linga* was set up here and remains one of the largest *Lingas* (phallicemblems) of Siva to be found and worshiped in India. The temple is still intact though the roof of the *Nat mandir* (Nat temple) attached to it has been replaced with corrugated iron-sheets.

Kamakhya Temple

The *Shakti* Temple of mother Goddess Kamakhya is situated on the top of Nilachal Hill. An important shrine of tantric Shaktism find mention in the inscription of the Allahabad pillar of Samudragupta. Devotees from all over India converge on this holy place during *Ambubashi* and *Manasha Puja*.

Saraighat Bridge

The first road cum rail bridge across the mighty Brahmaputra river is in Jalukbari connecting north and south bank. One can enjoy the scenic beauty of the hills and river water, migratory birds and relax at the Chilarai Park or Lachit Udyan, situated at both ends of the bridge.

Umananda

The great Shiva temple situated on the Peacock Island in the middle of the Brahmaputra in Guwahati attracts devotees from all over the country during Shiva Ratri. One can visit the temple by crossing the river by country boat plying from Kachari ghat. On the north bank of the

Brahmaputra, opposite Guwahati, where the third Pandava Arjun is believed to have watered his horse while undertaking journey during *Ashwamedh Yajna*.

Ashwaklanta

Ashwaklanta hillock is located in north Guwahati close to Doul Govinda. It is believed Lord Krishna stopped his chariot on his way to Rukmini Nagar to give rest to his tired horses. That is why it is *Ashwa, Klanta*. In later age, the temple of Shri Vishnu in eternal sleep and Shri Janardana were built on the hillock by the Ahom and the Koch kings. During British era, Viceroy Lord Curzon ordered repairing of the temple when the great earth quake of June 12, 1897 damaged these very badly. Shri Vishnu *Pada*, a foot print of Shri Vishnu is a holy spot on the margin of the river at the foothill where people use to perform *Pinda* ceremony of the dead ancestors more particularly on the auspicious day of *Ashokastami* in the month of *Chaitra*, a huge number of pilgrims visit the *Ashwaklanta* shrine after taking bath on the *Louhitya* (Brahmaputra). Their movement up and down the hillock from and to river side makes one wonder how deeply faith is rooted in human mind. The belief is that Holy Ganga flows upstream to this shrine on this particular day of the year. A little away from this hillock stands and islet named *Ar-Parvat* in the Brahmaputra as a wall blocking the view of the islet called *Karma Nasha*. It is said that a pilgrim after taking bath in Ashwaklanta *kunda* of the Lauhitya is not supposed to get the view of *Karma Nasha* which nullies *Punya* (virtues) earned by the pilgrim. In the famous battle of Saraighat, the Mughals set up at Aswaklanta hillock their assault base against the Ahom Army. This strategy was however foiled by the great Hero Lachit Barphukan, the Ahom General by thrustiny defeat on the Mughals. One can reach Ashwaklanta either by ferry service linked with the south bank or by road across the Saraighat Bridge.

Dirgheswari Temple

Located on the north bank of the Brahmaputra, this shrine is considered as one of the supreme Devi *Tirthas* of the state. Isolated and lying at the foot of a range of hills, it has several rock cut images which can be traced to the 11th to 12th century A.D. On the north of North Guwahati there is a hill named *Natuancha*. Here Lord Shiva and Goddess Parvoti and other Gods resided. This was alternative of *Kailash dham,* the abode of the Lord Shiva. Here *Beula*, the traditional chaste got her husband's life back by gaining a boon from Lord Shiva after pleasing him with her charming dance and music. The Dirgheswari *Dewalaya* in the Dirgheswari hill or *'Sita parbati'* exist beside this. The great hermit *Markanda* had his hermitage here. Lord Shiva also happered to carry on his shoulders his wife's dead body *(Sati)* over this site hills when one of Sati's limb fell here the Dirgheswari temple was built.

Manikarneswar

It is told in kalika puran that invaluable gems, pearls, gold, ruby and other precious stones were looted from beneathe the seas, the earth, underworld and from heaven by king Narakasur and he got them deposited in the shape of a mountain which is now known as Manikrneswar, where the king built a beautiful palace. In the Jogini tantra it has been extensively described as a reknown holy place. It is stated that in the 1st century a king called *Debesheswar* built a temple over *Manikarneswar Linga.*

This was ruined in the great earthquake and a new temple was erected during the reign of Ahom King Rajeswar Sinha in 1677. The temple seen at present in a dilapidated condition was broken in 1897. A Lake *Manikarna* once beautified the area but now it is in the bed of the Brahmaputra. Along with other celebrations *Shiva Ratri* festival is celebrated here with much religious fervor.

Kanai Barashi Boa

Kanai Barashi Boa is a huge rock said to have served Kanai, Lord Krishna as the seat for angling in the river as per legend. This site is only three minutes walk from the Doul Govinda temple premises. The recently established Anundo Ram Barooah Institute of Language Art & Culture is located close to the rock. This rock of unusual size bears evidence of the military might of this land in a two line script engraved thereon in old Assamese characters in their formative stage, which renders as *'The Turkis came to Kamrupa and got perished at this spot in the year 1206AD'*. This rock witnessed the victory of the Ahoms against the Mughal aggressors in the first battle on the Barnadi. Two Mohammadan Officers Sayed Chana and Sayed Firoz were taken prisoners and slain by the Ahom Generals, the *Buragohain* (Minister) and *Barphukan* (Viceroy) in cooperation with two other Ahom high ups and subsequently they got the Rangmohal *Garh* constructed along the bank of Rivulet Fulung (since dried up) to the foot hills of Dirgheswari hills. This old rampart (*Garh*) has served north Guwahati and the adjoining villages as an embankment cum road till this date.

Satra

Satra is one of the unique feature of Vaishnavism in Assam. It is an institution resembling to a certain extent, the Buddhist monastery system or the *matha* institution of the medieval period.

In north Guwahati there are satras – Auniati, Dihing and Garmur satra. All the satras have their head office in Majuli of upper Assam.

Madan Kamdev

Barely 40 kms. away from the sprawling metropolis Guwahati, on N.H. 52 Madan Kamdev is an enigma, a mystery, a marvel and in the words of Omar Khayam, "a veil past which I could not see". Very little is known about the origin of this magnificient archaeological ruins. Written history is almost silent on it, leaving wide room for conjectures and hypothesis. Kamrupa - the ancient name of Assam, is believed to have derived its name from the legend that love God Kama or Madan, after being turned into ashes by an angry Shiva, was reborn here. One school believes that Madan was reborn and united to Rati on this tiny hillock.

Hajo

Hajo is a sacred place for Hindus, Muslims and Buddhists. This unique heritage centre is 25km west of Guwahati and possess a place of pilgrimage for Muslims known as Poa-Mecca. It is believed that offering prayer here one can gain one fourth of the spiritual enlightenment which one can gain in Mecca. Hence it is *'poa'* meaning one fourth. The mosque was established by an Iraqi prince-turned-preacher, who traveled all the way to Assam in the 12th century to spread the Prophet's teachings. Among a large number of temples of Hajo, the chief being the Hayagriva-Madhab Temple. Hayagriva, king of the angels, resides at the top of the Manikuta hill. The present building of the temple was constructed by the Koch King Raghudevanarayan in 1583 A.D. after its demolition by Kala Pahar. However, the original temple was constructed, in all probability, in the 6th-7th century A.D. A section of scholars believe that the original temple was a Buddhist chaitya. Certain motifs of the original work, particularly a row of caparisoned elephants in high relief encircling the building appear to be specimens of Buddhist architecture. The elephant motif is identical to the decorative style of the cave temple at Ellora. There is another temple like building adjacent to the main temple called *'Doul Griha'* have been built by Ahom king Pramatta Singha in 1750 A.D.

There is a belief among a section of the Buddhist that Lord Buddha attained *nirvana* here. Large number of Bhutanese visit this temple every year during the winter season. At the same time it is a place of worship for the Hindus also. The temple is accessible via a long stone stairway. At the foot of the stairway is a large pond inhabited by one of Hajo's eminent residents: a giant turtle. Hajo is also renowned for its bell metal work.

Sualkuchi

Assam is known for three unique varieties of silks, the Golden *Muga*, the White *Pat* and the warm *Eri*. Silks grown all over the state find their way to Sualkuchi, 32 kms from Guwahati.

Sualkuchi is one of the world's largest traditional weaving villages often called the Manchester of the East. The entire population here is engaged in weaving exquisite silk fabrics. They are the caste population of Assam. This is a renowned centre of silk production, particularly known for *Muga* - the golden silk of Assam which is not produced anywhere else in the world.

Hira Potter

Assam has a tradition of terracotta and pot making which has been handed down from generation to generation. There are two traditional potter communities, the Hira and the Kumar. The Hira potters are residing in the Chaygaon area of Kamrup District barely a few kilometer from Guwahati.

The Hira Potters are probably the oldest potters in Assam who do not use the wheel at all in pottery making. They still use the primitive method of coiling. They manufacture household articles using the compression method. Among the Hiras, only the womenfolk are engaged in pottery making. The men folk help in procuring raw materials and selling the wares. The most commonly used pottery products including earthen pots and pitches, plates, incense stick holders, earthen lamps etc.

Doul Govinda Eco Museum : Paradigm and Prospects

Attempt has been made here to conceptualize an ecomuseum on the basis of its parameters. The concept of ecomuseum and the significance of the proposed territory has already been discussed. It has been observed that the concept of ecomuseum has been defined by different Museologists and it is also clear that an ecomuseum can not be developed in an insignificant space. The given territory for the ecomuseum must fulfill certain criterion. These criterions are the determinant of an ecomuseum site. Without these criterion or parameters a territory can be sanctified as an ecomuseum.

In this regard, site selected for experimentation of the concept of ecomuseum is the Doul Govinda sacred complex. Here, attempt shall be made to find out the existence of required parameters (as indicated by the western Museologists) in the given territory of Doul Govinda so as to explain how these parameters gets fit into this sacred complex and can be the proper perspectives of an ecomuseum.

The **parameters** prescribed by western Museologists has been discussed below –

Geographical scale

The scale of an ecomuseum very much depends on its interpretation of the nature and extent of territory. Few scholars view that ecomuseum should cover a wide area. However ecomuseums can exist on a small geographical scale, too, promoting a single site or a discrete town, village. Every museum, be it an ecomuseum, national, regional or local museum or a conventional museum, but has a territory. For the traditional museum it is the concept of geographical territory that helps to define its collecting policies and target a particular group of population. This territory often equates with political boundaries and also the sources of financial support. The ecomuseum concept of territory is different where it can more readily be beyond the artificial boundaries imposed by authority and select territory that are limited by for example, topography, dialect, architecture, history or economy. It is therefore the nature of the concept of territory that enables to distinguish between ecomuseum and traditional museum. Ecomuseum can work at any scale that is considered most beneficial and most appropriate. An ecomuseum on a limited geographical scale perhaps helping a small local community to establish its identity and promoting development is just as valid an approach as one that covers hundreds of square kilometers and is geared to sustainable tourism.

In the context of the present study, if we would like to consider the political boundary, the territory of the proposed museum will be restricted up to three surrounding villages of Doul Govinda complex the Rajaduar, Madhyamkhanda & Shilsako. But from the point of view of the principles of Ecomuseum, considering both tangible and intangible heritage associated with the sacred complex it will cover a wide range & the spots that are included in the heritage trail, reflects the territory which is much beyond the political boundary. The political boundary of the sacred complex is the core area. But a particular ecomuseum specially the Doul Govinda ecomuseum influence beyond the three villages. The influence may be of religious, cultural and social. Through the religious influence the museum will attract the devotees from different parts of Assam. The social and cultural influence may even go beyond the Kamrup district.

Interpreting selected environments in the cultural landscape – in situ conservation

The idea of the in situ preservation and interpretation of sites does appear to hold true for most ecomuseums. It is real ecomuseum indicator. The majority of ecomuseums have a central administrative base and a number of dispersed sites that together attempt to portray a holistic view of their region.

However ecomuseums are not the only organization involved with in situ conservation and interpretation. In many protected areas in the United Kingdom and USA interpretive strategies are based around such an approach.

The Doul Govinda sacred complex works as 'Head Quarter' (after Corsane and Holleman)[3] in reference to present study. The antennas will be the different heritage spots that are the centers of both tangible and intangible heritage.

---

3 Corsane and Holleman (1993: 111-25) suggest that the ecomuseum incorporates a much larger territory in a fairly open ended manner. Here, the territory is not simply defined in a geographical or administrative term, but rather as any whole unit where the inhabitants share a common way of life, culture, occupation or traditional custom. Run from a central headquarters the comuseum has a series of 'antennae' within the territory of the museum. These antennae form a network through which the activities of information gathering, research, display and education can be performed.

For instance, different heritage sites, community around those sites will be made involve to preserve their heritage. The Hira potters, who have the unique tradition of making hand made pottery, the weavers of Sualkuchi, who are the producer of Assam Silk. The community involve with these age-old tradition will be aware of their heritage and they will also put effort to preserve their tradition by continuing the practice.

Interpreting what, where and how – preserving, restoring and reconstructing

There is no substantive difference between the role of the ecomuseum and the traditional museum when considering the basic functions of interpretations and conservation.

Both types of organization are attempting to preserve fragments of the heritage which may be a site, monument, an object, a rare breed or examples of local oral tradition and help people to understand its significance. What is really important here is where the interpretation or conservation is carried out and how it is achieved. Interpretation should be site based, so demonstrating the significance of place and conservation or restoration should reflect a commitment from the local community to its heritage. All the activities of eco museum including conservation and restoration are supported by local community. The eco museum of St. Degan is an excellent example of ecomuseum features where interpretation is based around farm buildings that have preserved in *situ* and carried out by local guides.

In site interpretation is more effective and interesting rather that de-centralizing the objects or site and interpreting. Here, the devotees of Doul Govinda sacred complex, can experience the sacred performances & can observe the activities of the sacred specialists. There are volunteers in the complex who can interpret those too thus enhancing the site based interpretation.

Activating the visitor and making the cultural heritage accessible

Ecomuseum encourages the visitor to travel beyond the walls of the museum and experience a wide range of cultural and natural heritage sites. 'Activation' is the reflection of the desire of the ecomuseum to create a link – a spiritual and personal one – between the visitor and the environment, between the visitor and the region, to try and convey the elusive concept that is a 'sense of place' (Davis:1999:222). Taking the museum beyond the walls and the boundaries of conventional ownership, therefore, appears to be an important ecomuseum characteristic. This is in direct contrast to most traditional museums, which rarely interpret sites beyond the museum and have little to do with sites for which they are not immediately responsible.

The proposed ecomuseum will enable the visitors to visit different heritage centers spotted in different parts of Guwahati. These will create a link between the visitors and the centers, in other words a sense of place. Visitors can interact with the centers which will lead to active participation of the visitors with both the tangible & intangible heritage associated with there. A visitor will enjoy the scenic beauty of Vasisthashram , can experience the influence of nine planets predicted by astrologers in Navagraha, can learn the technique of hand made pottery from Hira potters and can run a spinning shuttle with the weavers of Sualkuchi.

Ecomuseums are founded on the interaction between culture and tourism

Politics and economics influence museums and the financial requirement of any museum is considerable. Therefore justifying the launch of a new ecomuseum initiative requires the preparation of a carefully constructed business plan as well as the adoption of a particular philosophical paradigm. For pragmatic reasons new eco museums have therefore tended to follow the Scandinavian model that identifies a strong link with tourism and its associated economic benefits.

As mentioned, though it is a Scandinavian concept, yet tourism can not be ignored in the context of proposed ecomuseum, Tourism industry is growing in north -east very fast. So, by including this ecomuseum in the tourist itinerary, the museum and community involved can boost up from all aspects including the economy.

Ecomuseums are based on the joint efforts of local authorities, associations, organizations and private individuals

The ecomuseums are usually a cooperative venture. This is specially true while considering the sources of financial support. However this is an indication that the ecomuseum plays an important role as a catalyst to joint initiatives. The description tends to support that this role is specially responsible for sites in large geographical areas that frequently straddle administrative boundaries. Ekomuseum Bergslagen is a good example of cooperative venture supported by seven administrative districts, two major museums and two tourist boards.

Doul Govinda ecomuseum will be a joint venture of Doul Govinda management committee, volunteers and local youth associations. The ecomuseum will also be under the supervision of Block Development Department of North Guwahati, as it is the government body that undertakes all the development work of the region. The members of the body get democratically elected. Though ecomuseum denies the existence of conventional museum, yet here in this case, Assam State Museum plays an important role. As the tangible heritage of this region has been preserved here, this museum is also considered as an important organs of Doul Govinda ecomuseum (details discussed earlier). Thus, government departments will also be a part of the venture. Besides, different NGO's who are working for the preservation of rich cultural heritage of Assam will contribute a lot. *Kamrup Anusandhan Samiti*, pioneer in establishing Assam State Museum can join their hand. Anando Ram Barua Library and Research Center, a center for preservation of folk heritage in Doul Govinda ecomuseum territory can be the resource center. The effort of Assam Tourism will also be an added advantage.

Ecomuseums are dependent on active voluntary efforts

Volunteers exist in case of most of the ecomuseums. Most museums use volunteers for a wide range of purpose, including documentation, research, curatorial activities, visitor survey etc. One important point to be noted here that volunteers are integral part of ecomuseum. If volunteers withdraw support from conventional museum, the museum can survive. But there are instances when ecomuseum gets closed due to lack of commitment from volunteers. Ecomusee St Degan, France is a good example which is entirely run by volunteers, the members of the association that was formed in 1969 being totally responsible for the administration, management and interpretation of the site. Similarly, Ecomusee d Alsace use some 150 volunteers to assist with the varied activities on the site.

The contribution of volunteers play an important role in Doul Govinda temple. There are already large number of volunteers working in the temple and helping the day to day activities associated with it. There are potentialities among the youths of the region who can offer their support to run the ecomuseum smoothly. They are well versed with their local traditions and that is how they can interpret their heritage in an easy manner and also that effort will make them aware of their heritage and its preservation.

Ecomuseum aim to make a little known space accessible to tourists

Ecomuseums have emerged in places that are trying to assert their cultural identity, that they are places with a low tourists profile. In such cases creation of an ecomuseum could be seen as one way to make a place better known to the wider world. In other words, places that are little known are still of tremendous significance to the people who live there. Places may be little known for a number of reasons, including geographical remoteness, poor communications or that they are beyond the normal purview of the tourist. Thus many small industrial regions fall into this category simply because they are not normally identified as pleasant places to visit. Because of this reason we find many ecomuseums in remote rural areas or in those that have a significant industrial past or lie on the margins of society.

The proposed ecomuseum site is in north Guwahati of Assam. Guwahati is divided into two parts by the river Brahmaputra. The Southern bank of Guwahati has become now the residence of multi-ethnic group and accordingly has undergone tremendous changes, Comparatively North Guwahati still remains intact. There is no such industry or other center of commerce. The area is less developed as the river has made it little remote. Therefore, this part is little known and focused. Establishment of an ecomuseum in this bank, which will also include some centres of south bank will make the whole ecomuseum territory better known to all.

The ecomuseums appeals to local inhabitants in an effort to create a feeling of local identity

The significance of local identity is central to the philosophy of ecomuseum and an important indicator of ecomuseum. It actively involves people in creating their own identity. By doing so it encourages their involvement in the region's heritage so leading to a greater understanding of local cultural identity.

The proposed ecomuseum will create a sense of identity of the community around and will create a sense of belongingness.

Ecomuseums appeals to schools and education at all levels

Ecomuseums plays a significant role as institutions for lifelong learning. Due to its in situ interpretation nature, people of all the age groups can get the benefit of learning. This statement on ecomuseum is however not exclusive to ecomuseum in present day context. Conventional museums were not concern for education for all. But now a days the statement has changed. Conventional museums have dedicated educational programs aimed at all age groups and to all levels of ability.

After visiting the proposed ecomuseum school children will be able to learn practically, what they read in their school books. They can gain knowledge of the society they are living. The museum will also educate people of all groups. In other words, the museum will be a non-conventional institute of education. However, this role of museum is applicable to both traditional and ecomuseum. Traditional museum have also started conducting education programmes for all type of target visitors. Therefore, this parameters can not be exclusive for the proposed museum.

The ecomuseum is a continuous process of evolution, where new features and improvements both long term and short term are introduced into the development programme

The statement brings a distinction between traditional and ecomuseums too. Ecomuseums are free to develop its activities whatever the way it is beneficial for the local community. They are also free from the boundaries of rigid local government control, which also makes easier to take action and to adopt new ideas. The territorial nature of ecomuseum provides several options for development like the ability to acquire or interpret new sites or address new themes, whereas traditional museums have to restrict themselves to the museums building and their permanent collection. However traditional as well as ecomuseums can be innovative not only in terms of physical improvement to a building but also in their strategies.

The proposed ecomuseum hence can enhance the local community to adopt such strategies which will help in the growth and development of their socio economic and religious life. The museum will be under the local authority so there will not be any hassles from government authority. The nature of such strategies can be for example, adoption of a new site in the heritage trail of the museum. There are so many areas around north Guwahati where we find remains of Ahom rulers. So adoption of such a site will bring into light many new aspects of Assam history and the community around the area will also be made aware of their heritage they have inherited and to take care of that. Thus, the ecomuseum can continuously carry on the process and introduce many development programme.

Ecomuseums aim to show the whole – from general to the specific

A holistic approach to the interpretation of the cultural and natural heritage of a defined territory is central to the ecomuseum concept. The implication of such an approach is that as many different sites as possible should be interpreted and that interconnections between the sites and between culture and nature are fully explained. It also implies that the whole story is available to every visitor irrespective of his or her age or educational background that the holistic principle should be applied to the consumer as well as resource. The holistic approach requires the removal of barriers between academic disciplines and stories and themes being developed which interweave specialist knowledge. If all these criteria are met, then the ecomuseum visitor can fully experience and understand the special nature of individual places. There is no doubt that the fragmented nature of ecomuseum sites and the fact that they are often interlinked gives the ecomuseum tremendous potential to promote holistic interpretation. Many of them have achieved this with considerable flair. For example, Sexial, Portugal is a special place because of its proximity to major rivers and the sea, everything about the region is linked in some way to the maritime world. Its suit of sites, including tide mills, shipyards, Roaman sites and a small palace. All are interpreted in relation to the sea and maritime trade, while its restored vessels enable the visitor to experience the estuarine and river environment firsthand. It is difficult for traditional museums to reach this level of holistic interpretation, even though some of them are taking steps to dismantle long cherished barriers between disciplines.

The establishment of an ecomuseum is North Guwahati will be a holistic approach that will lead to interpretation of all the tangible and intangible heritage of the territory. The different heritage centers covered under heritage trail will be interlinked; thereby a network will get created. This network will enable visitors of all age groups to experience the diverse features of the rich heritage of the territory.

Ecomuseums collaborate with artists, craftsmen, writers, actors and musicians

Many ecomuseums are devoted to rural crafts, agriculture, industrial processes and maritime history and document the intangible heritage (oral tradition, music, folklore etc) in addition to sites and objects. The interpretation of such resources while using traditional techniques such as labels or guided tours is made more meaningful and enjoyable by observing craftsmen, 'living history' events and listening to live music. Many of the ecomuseums described earlier make full use of such skills and many of the larger museums employ people full time during the tourists season to enable better interpretation and provide an all round experience. However many conventional museums like open air museum or site museums also provide space for crafts demonstration and make people experience the reality.

The Doul Govinda ecomuseum will inspire not only the people to keep their heritage intake but also the artisans and craftsmen. The museum will be a collaborative institution. Along with the interlinks with different heritage centres, it will enhance the artisans involved to be more productive and curious. The craftsmen demonstrating their skill can create 'living history'. Though many traditional museum have crafts of Doul Govinda ecomuseum, it will be a different experience . In the crafts demonstration area of traditional museum everything is re-created and tried to give a sense of reality in a best possible way , but taking a round of the whole area or village of a particular craftsmen is more effective and interesting feelings. For example, a visitor of Doul Govinda ecomuseum can experience the technique of Assam silk in Sualkuchi area. Sualkuchi is Asia's largest village where every household have their, weaving workshop. By visiting the village one can watch the craft and also can meet the artisans involved along with the knowledge of socio-cultural life of the people. In other words the ecomuseum will be a collaborative effort of artisans.

The ecomuseum promotes research by means of study circles and at an academic level

This statement proved correct with many Scandinavian ecomuseums. These museums have brought together groups of local individuals and encouraged them to research a particular aspect of their area. The research is usually related to a site, a process or an individual. The Ecomusee du Fier Monde in Montreal has adopted a similar approach in Canada, with local people working as a team to investigate the lost histories of local industries and the people who worked in them. Such 'study circles' are however not found in all ecomuseums. The volume of such academic work compared to conventional museum is also very few.

A study circle can be created including the local youth and other learned person. The study circle can conduct research on individual for example. North Guwahti has produced several renowned personalities of Assam. Anando Ram Barua, who was a scholar and first ICS Officer of Assam. So, research on him can reveal many unknown aspect of his philosophy. Besides individual, the researcher can investigate different aspect associated with Brahmaputra river, its history and also the flora, fauna found on the river bed. This river is a legend for the people of north Guwahati territory, so different myths and folk tales involved with the river can be revealed.

The ecomuseum aims to illustrate the connection between nature and culture, between past and present, between then and now

This statement once gain expresses the holistic nature of the ecomuseum and its role in conserving the past for use in the present. Ecomuseums have played a very significant role in conserving fragment of history, making it accessible and promoting understanding. Every ecomuseum without exception seeks to create a link between the past and the present.

The proposed ecomuseum can illustrate connection between people of the territory and the Brahmaputra river. How the river has shaped the life and culture of the people. In fact the river has influenced the food habit, dresses, in other words every aspect of their life.

Exclusive Parameters

Above mentioned are some of the important parameters of ecomuseum. However, evaluation of significance of potential ecomuseums parameters is inconclusive primarily because of variety of ways in which the ecomuseum has evolved. Ecomuseums also share certain characteristics with conventional museums. Again some ecomuseum may share a character, others do not. For instance, some ecomuseums promote economic development via tourism and others do not, some may promote and publish research work but not all. Despite this varied nature, Peter Davis has identified following exclusive parameters of ecomuseums (Davis, 1999: 228) –

- The adoption of a territory that is not necessarily defined by conventional boundaries.
- The adoption of a 'fragmented site' policy which is linked to in situ conservation and interpretation.
- Conventional vies of site ownership are abandoned, conservation and interpretation of sites via liaison and cooperation.
- The empowerment of local communities; the involvement of local people in museum activities and in the creation of their cultural identity.
- The potential for interdisciplinary and holistic interpretation.

If we evaluate the above exclusive features suggested by Davis in the context of present study, it appear, Doul Govinda sacred complex ecomuseum site mark a territory which is not demarcated by political boundary and it covers a wide range of region. The details have already been discussed under the parameter – *Geographical scale*. For in situ conservation, Doul Govinda has been adopted as head quarter and other heritage centers as antennas. The proposed ecomuseum will be the joint venture of Doul Govinda management committee, north Guwahati block development department, local volunteers and others. The proposed ecomuseum will be by the people, for the people and of the people and have immense potential for holistic interpretation. The details of these parameters have been discussed already. Thus, the proposed ecomuseum site fulfills the exclusive criterions or parameters of ecomuseums suggested by Peter Davis.

Patrik Boylan produced a similar list of characteristics that allows museums to measure how 'ecomuseological' they are (Boylan, 1992: 29-30). His five key concepts were

- Territory
- Fragmentation and the nature of ecomuseum 'collections'
- Interdisciplinary approaches to interpretation
- The nature of the ecomuseum 'customer'
- Local democracy and community empowerment.

He suggested that if each of these five characteristics is ranked on a scale from 1 (traditional approach) to 5 (ecomuseum approach), then a score of 13 or below indicates a traditional museum, 14-19 is an outgoing community centered museum with an interest in the environment and a score of 20+ identifies a true ecomuseum. He is of the opinion that tested against this scale many organizations that call themselves ecomuseums would fall within the center category (that is, they are not really ecomuseums). Peter Davis supported this ranking system. He said that this ranking might be considered a measurement of the amount of overlap between museum, environment and community. However he also suggests that anyone looking at ecomuseums with an unprejudiced eye could only conclude that they demonstrate a very significant amount of variation.

Let us now evaluate the proposed Doul Govinda ecomuseum site and experiment how 'ecomuseological' it is from the point of view of Boylan. The museum fulfills all the characteristics suggested by Boylan. The museum includes a specific territory, its heritage centres are scattered upto a wide area and the museum is represented by Assamese community. Thus the proposed ecomuseum can gain a score of 20+ which also proves to be a true ecomuseum.

Doul Govinda Eco Museum Preserving Local Identity

Ecomuseums are at their very essence 'hoilistic' in approach and it is just this emphasis on the importance of the whole and the interdependence of its parts that allows a response to a context that is multi layered in terms of existing and impending cultural damage. Indeed, through this lens, the philosophy of the ecomuseum paradigm and the proposed context are conterminous.

That is why the local identity of the proposed territory of Doul Govinda sacred complex is need to preserve and setting up of an ecomuseum can be the best measure for the preservation.

Local Identity

Local identity is key term in the concept of ecomuseum. UNESCO defines local identity as the correspondence between a community (national, ethnic, linguistic etc.) and its cultural life, as well as the right of each community to its own culture.

Although UNESCO has provided a workable definition of cultural identity it is evident that the term identity, cultural identity and community are regularly used in a seemingly interchangeable manner in museological literature. Identity has become increasingly popular as an expressive term for the need to find stability and order in a rapidly changing world. Hall prefers to use the term identification rather than identity, suggesting that this reflects recognition of some common origin or shared characteristics with another person or group or with an ideal and with the natural closure of solidarity and allgiance established in this foundation. He also suggested that identification can be won or lost, sustained or abandoned. In other words, identity is not fixed, but changes with time and circumstances. Argument as to whether identity is rooted in geographic locality, nation, politics, religion, education, ethnic background or genealogy are not relevant of course, but it is important to recognize that they are dynamic not concrete factors. Even ethnicity can be diluted. Circumstances which influence a cultural identity based on territory including the dominance of certain cultural groups, migration, the formation of new societal groupings and communications technology are part of this dynamic.

When we define cultural identity in the context of museums, it is apparent that issues relating to the ownership of major cultural objects and the representation of other culture will continue to debate. In 1982, in a meeting in Mexico city, a major statement was prepared by UNESCO – the declaration on cultural policies, which clearly illustrates how the concept of cultural identity is incorporated into global cultural policy. The key paragraphs in this document make a useful summary of the significance of the meaning of cultural identity for museums although it inevitably has a 'national' emphasis; many of the points made are relevant to communities at every scale:

- Every culture represents a unique and irreplaceable body of values since each people's traditions forms of expression are its most effective means of demonstrating its presence in the world.
- The assertion of cultural identity therefore contributes to the liberation of peoples. Conversely, any form of domination constitutes a denial or the impairment of that identity.
- Cultural identity is a treasure that vitalizes mankind's possibilities of self fulfillment by moving every people and every group to seek nurture in its past to welcome contributions from outside that are compatible with its own characteristics and so to continue the process of its own creation.
- All cultures form part of the common heritage of mankind. The cultural identity of a people is enriched through contact with the traditions and values of others. Culture is dialogue the exchange of ideas and experiences and the appreciation of other values and traditions it withers and dies in isolation.

Georges Henry Riviere, who is considered as pioneer in the evolution of the concept of ecomuseum, defined and redefined ecomuseum three times. His definition portrays emphasis on local identity. His definition includes many of the key concepts like, local identity, territory, landscape, a sense of history and community, which are important in creating a sense of belonging.

The significance of local identity is central to the philosophy of the ecomuseum and is undoubtedly an important ecomuseum indicator. However it should be stressed that the ecomuseum does not simply appeal to local inhabitants, it is not simply a matter of purveying a view of local identity for consumption by local people but a process that should actively involve them in creating their own identity. The efforts of Ekomuseum Bergslagen to involve local people in all its activities by running education days, seminars, lectures and meetings is a good example of the ways in which an ecomuseum can make contact with its communities. By doing so it encourages their involvement in the region's heritage, so leading to a greater understanding of local cultural identity. This proactive approach is one way in which we might distinguish an ecomuseum from a traditional museum. Although the best ecomuseums have permanent staff, there must be active co-operation between them and local people if the ecomuseum ideal is to be achieved. The ecomuseum movement is characterized by an idealistic and humanistic philosophy, including the concept of a symbiotic relationship between professional museum staff and local people. It also has an educational vision that provides ordinary people with an opportunity to define and build their own cultural identity. Traditional museums although also seeking to encapsulate the attributes of a locality are not always so keen to encourage community participation.

Local Identity of Doul Govinda Ecomuseum Territory

When we talk of the local identity of the people of the Doul Govinda ecomuseum territory, it includes all the tangible and intangible heritage associated with it. Here to be mentioned that the natural settings and the river ecology of this territory also plays a vital role. The tangible and intangible heritage of the territory has been discussed already. It can be summarized that the local identity of the people of this territory is very strong and significant. They carry a rich cultural heritage, which are reflected in every aspect of their life ranging from religious, social, cultural, historical, archaeological or ecological.

This rich and unique identity of the people of this territory is now reflecting very vast and rapid changes. Changes and developments are continuous process and the process which can not be ignored. Instead, it is required to extract the positive effects of that and get acquainted. Till few years ago, north Guwahati was known as a place which occupies a significant place in Assam history and possess some noteworthy material evidence of the ruled and the rulers of this region. The region was also famous as it has produced some brain child of Assam. This northern bank of the river Brahmaputra was connected through fairy services, one had to cross the river Brahmaputra to reach here. Very limited number of state government bus ply everyday to this bank after crossing the Saraighat bridge. The connecting road was in terrible state and people usually avoided that bus service. The faculty higher secondary school was on this bank. So students of southern bank were brought by school bus but students of upper classes had to avail the fairy service. Dominant number of household were agro based, had sufficient number of land to use. However families living close to the bank had to suffer from flood. Parents were aware of educating their children, so, school drop out or illiteracy was lesser to include. The male folk were mainly on service and used to come to the south Guwahati to attend their office. Female folk mainly concentrated on their household chores, rearing children and were engaged in weaving or producing other handicraft materials during their leisure times. Business was not an occupation preferred to survive and villagers were interdependent to live a smooth life. The concept of hotel or guest house of renting property or any business establishment was almost zilch. Any religious or traditional observance was a means to get villagers united and celebrate. Except the devotees to Doul Govinda temple north Guwahati rarely received any outside guest. Out of those devotees few would visit other heritage centres like Ashwaklanta or Dirgheswari, otherwise the regular prayer or worships takes place in these centres and those were restricted to the residents of the region only. Interference of government administration or other organizations were limited.

The above picture of the territory is altering very fast. The concept of urbanization and assimilation has influenced a lot. One of the major cause of this change is the establishment of the Indian Institute of

Technolgy (IIT) Guwahati chapter in this northern bank of the river Brahmaputra. This is a première educational establishment helping the students of specially north east to become the proud of nation by acquiring the knowledge of science and technology. The institute occupy a vast land of this bank, though regular operation has already started, yet construction still going on. The institute authority has started hiring local people giving employment opportunity to the youth. It has become now eye opener for the people who are yet to get engaged in any government service. They have adopted business as their means of livelihood. Many small and big shops have come up, restaurant, guest house, paying guest facility, all have been made available. People have started renting their house to the outsiders who have been absorbed in the Institute but yet to get any official accommodation. Many labourers who work in the construction or other activities associated with the institute have adopted north Guwahati as their new residence. The natural beauty, fresh air and easy access of fresh eatables have applauded outsiders who have grown up in urban settings so far. Once connected with only fairy service, north Guwahati today is easy access from any part of Assam. Those terrible mud lanes of north Guwahati no more exists. Today in every five minutes there will be tracker service to any lane and corners of north Guwahati. With the government aid and easy loan facility many local youth could make trackers available as local conveyance. Gas agency, petrol pump etc are some other new addition to this region. In other words, establishment IIT Guwahati in north Guwahati is another way bring changes to the lives of the people here.

Besides IIT, establishment of a technology park in Amingaon, adjacent to Doul Govinda territory has also contributed for the rapid changes of this region. Many other small industries have come up. A container industry establishment was in fact recently bought some controversy too. Tourism industry in Assam has boost up. It has included the heritage centres of north Guwahati in their tourists itinerary. It has made people aware of their heritage and local people have come out with many development projects and helping tourism to grow up fast. Many non government organizations (NGO) have started working for the welfare of people of the region. Students have gone even abroad for higher studies, they are no more restricted to only northern bank of river Brahmaputra. Many personalities who hails from north Guwahati but have studied outside and gained experience now wants to take up development project of the region and have started contributing for their betterment.

The natural atmosphere of the region has got effected also. The open sky and fresh air of the region is now under smoke and other deteriorating agents causing pollution. Introduction of new machinery is causing both atmospheric as well as noise pollution. The trackers that ply continuously have become threat to the health of the residents and also to flora and fauna.

Above changes that taking place in case of economy, communication, occupation etc. have ultimately effected the day to day life of the people and hence effecting overall the culture. The traditions, beliefs, practices, rituals, art, in other words, in every sphere of life has undergone changes. At the outset it is to be mentioned that in spite of the changes, people of this region still the follower of Lord Doul Govinda. Their emotions attached to the temple is not been hampered due to any external enforcement. This is the unique feature of the people of this territory. People still make it a daily activity to visit the temple once in a day, offer any first product of their kitchen garden to it and also put effort to volunteer any job related to the temple. They still believe Lord Doul Govinda is there with them and they are surviving only with His blessings. Because of this unique emotional attachment that Doul Govinda sacred complex has been considered as the 'head office' of the present study on perspective ecomuseum site.

Changes prominent in their traditions. Though Doul Govinda is a neo vaishnavite temple, people believe in saivite sect also. The same group of people who visit Doul Govinda, found worshipping in nearby satra also and also they get engaged in celebrating *Durga Puja* following shaktism tradition. People have become more outgoing and modern and have started ignoring their traditions. Easy access to urban hub of south Guwahati has indulged people in some bad practice also, youth are no more ignorant of foreign wine or other food habit. Life style has changed.

Women folk find it more convenient to buy their clothes and other necessities from market, because fancy bazaar, which is considered as main market of Guwahati, is very well connected with north Guwahati now. One do not require to cross the Brahmaputra by fairy, instead, they just pay Rs. 5/- and reach fancy bazaar. So the age old tradition of weaving clothes is not a common practice now and they have started adopting other dresses than their traditional *mekhela chadar*. Food habit has changed. Having a kitchen garden is not priority for every house hold. Easy communication has helped business man from southern bank to sell their products there. In IIT, there are employees from different parts of the country, so business man have to consider their needs equally. Hence, new goods have been introduced and have become daily need of original inhabitants too.

As mentioned earlier changes are not always harmful, but every society equally has to restrict itself to a certain limit. The limit which do not effects its roots. If we observe the changes in north Guwahati, it has both positive and negative impact. Changes taking place and people have become more conscious and developed, so this is definitely a good progress. But the changes which is turning the society to a different phase is really a matter to be taken seriously. This is not true that north Guwahati never experienced any change before. It is equally true that people of north Guwahati has adopted many customs which earlier were not known to them. After all every society is under the continuous process of change. But recently north Guwahati is showing very fast process of change. Being very close to urban settings of southern Guwahati, north Guwahati maintained its unique feature of combination of traditionality with modernity. This unique feature is under threat now and loosing gradually its firm root. This is now a matter of time that north Guwahati converts into an urban hub.

The ecomuseum as a rescue mechanism for local identity

The decades long forced atrophy of north Guwahati cultural landscapes, both physical and societal presents a context for which rescue mechanisms are imperative. It is clear that a holistic approach to the rescue of cultural landscapes is vital, one that engages unequivocally with the community living in north Guwahati. Ecomuseums have the potential plasticity to reach out with a solution to the layers of cultural damage in the region. This universality in scope in linked to the notion of the 'total' environment that plays a key role in the paradigm. Indeed the 'eco' in ecomuseum has been posited to denote an environment which 'can be said to embrace both natural and human aspects within a very intricate and interconnected system. The network encompasses both biophysical features and those elements which have been manipulated, modified or constructed by man as well as intangibles such as economic, social, cultural and political dimensions which are also an integral part of the human environment' (Corsane and Holleman: 1993: 114)

It can also be argued that the ecomuseum model has responded successfully to contexts with parallel to that of south east Turkey. The model's key protagonist Hughes de Varine (Bedekar, 1995:XIV) has flagged up its usefulness in tackling problems of cultural identity and self reliance in countries with difficult majority or minority balances. Indeed, during its evolutional period embedded within new museology in the 1970's and 1980's, the paradigm tapped into the cultural needs of minority communities and has since emerged with some frequency near borders and minority cultures. The Basque Country for example, located on the French Spanish border and home to a community of three million united by the ancient language of Euskera has seen museums, including ecomuseums, flourish following the commencement of democratic processes in the late 1970's. of the 60 museums located there, 44 were post Franco. Many ecomuseums have been promoted by the Basque government and used as tools to recover identity.

Ecomuseums are also often responses to local rallying and mobilization against threat to cultural or natural heritage. Peter Davis (Davis,1999 :101) has linked the foundation of ecomuseums in numerous places around the world to struggle to situations where communities and the material culture of their past have come under threat and sites the Ecomusee du Larzac in France. This ecomuseum in the moonlike causse landscape came into being as a result of a waged by local people to resist the planned large scale extension of a military camp. Mobilization against threat is happening pell-mell in south east Turkey with local groups desperate to save cultural landscapes from inundation. These could be vital example to implement in Doul Govinda. Local gathering, rallying or mobilization are some of the ways by which the threatened cultural and natural landscape can rescued in a sufficient manner.

The ecomuseum also privileges collective memory. Rivard (1988:53) determines that 'New Museology dictates that the collective memory must be used as a resource and quotes Max Querrrien's observation that the ecomuseum's 'true heritage is nothing other than the collective memory from which it derives an identity that in its singular nature is caught up with present history and the building of the future. This utilization of collective memory of the local populations by ecomuseums have resonance for people of north Guwahati who are loosing their folk traditions due to the intervention of other culture. Here to be mentioned that collective memory is the history, folklore, tradition, customs and behaviour pattern of a given community. In the very concept of ecomuseum the tangible space percolates to the intangible one. That means history merges with folklore or the folk expression to give it a holistic meaning to the every elements of the social, cultural and natural properties of a given territory. This collective memory is one of the form of intangible heritage. The UNESCO could give a provisional definition to the intangible heritage in 2001 and in 2003 instituted the Convention for Safeguarding of the intangible cultural heritage (World Heritage Convention) subsequently ICOM took the cue from the UNESCO and declared 'Museums and Intangible Heritage' as the theme of the International Museum Day in 2004. ICOM later on decided to deliberate on the same theme in 20th ICOM Triennially in Seoul in 2004. These events obviously brings into focus the concern of the human society towards the intangible heritage. Unfortunately a large chunk of which has already been lost in the progress of human history. And now in 21st century globalization has brought a challenge for the countries having traditional base in the realm of intangible heritage.

It is clear that the ecomuseum could be a vehicle to safeguard the cultural continuity of the Doul Govinda sacred complex territory. Given not only the central, democratic role in museum action played by locals in the paradigm but also recognizing that in a context of assimilation and repression, the people themselves would be their own greatest advocates in respecting identity and the responsibility in a changing society for the conservation of their age old tradition by revival and retrieval. The ecomuseum has the advantage of dealing with collective memory and the awareness among the villagers about their rich possession that is collective memory is most convenient method. This is being another advantage of ecomuseum as rescue mechanism.

A sense of distinctiveness of place, the essence of an ecomuseum and a recognition of the value and significance of heritage at a local level both posited as ecomuseum enabling conditions by Corsane are both held particularly strongly in this particular site of north Guwahati. Heritage centres like Dirgheswari or Ashwaklanta or Manikarneswar are full of cultural markers for the people of north Guwahati. It was the doorway for King, administrative head for rulers or sometimes a center for shakti worship and so on and so forth are the subject of many local stories.

It can be hence concluded that ecomuseum is one of best possible mechanism to conserve the lost glory of the unique Assamese tradition that exist until few years ago. Indeed, the very concept of the ecomuseum is conservation oriented. It is a total initiative by people's action. One of the objectives of the ecomuseum have been identified as the local identity. Local identity could also be interlinked with conservation. The local identity in ecomuseum set up is territory based and partly dependent on the history and archaeology. Tangible heritage materials in terms of history and archaeology are immensely complemented by tradition, language, customs, beliefs and practices and art having root in the given territory. When we talk about the conservation of the local identity we indirectly mean the conservation of the intangible heritage.

A conventional museum as a matter fact could be identified with the conservation of heritage of the past. In the context of Doul Govinda territory that role is being played by Assam State Museum, Guwahati. Even the museum dealing with the contemporary life style can not escape conservation need of the society in terms of heritage in totality. But these are physical part of conservation and carried out by all types of conventional museums. Preventive heritage conservation is a new dimension in a world of globalization which is addressed in ecomuseum dealing with the intangible materials. So establishment of an ecomuseum in Doul Govinda sacred complex will be the mechanism for the conservation of the intangible heritage of the territory. Conservation of tangible part can also be undertaken and conventional museums are restricted with that. Ecomuseums have the advantage of both. This is how in a prospective site like Doul Govinda sacred complex of north Guwahati establishment of an ecomuseum will encourage to play a pivotal role for the conservation of the endangered rich cultural heritage (both tangible and intangible) of the territory.

References

Barua, B.K., *Cultural History of Assam*, Guwahati, 2003

Barua, Krishnamurti, *Karmajogi Prafulla Ch. Barooah*, Guwahati, 1992

Barua, P.C., 'North Guwahati where Time has Stood Still', *The Assam Tribune*, Guwahati, 1985

Bedekar, V.H., *New Museology for India*, New Delhi, 1995

Boylan, Ptrick 'Ecomuseums and the new museology – some definitions', *Museum Journal* 92(4), London, 1992

Chaudhury, R.D., *Sculptural Heritage of Assam*, Janpath, 2000

Corsane, G. and Holleman, W. 'Ecomuseums: a brief evaluation', *Museums and the Environment*, Pretoria, 1993

Das, B.M., *The People of Assam*, Delhi, 1968

Davis, P., *Ecomuseums A Sense of Place*, London and New York, 1999

Dutt,K.N. (ed.), *Aspects of the Heritage of Assam*, Guwahati, 1959

Gait, Edward, *A History of Assam*, Guwahati, 2001

Neog, Maheswar, *Sankaradeva*, Delhi, 1967

Vidyarthi, L.P., *The Sacred Complex of Hindu Gaya*, Bombay, 1961

Vidyarthi, L.P. et.el, *The Sacred Complex of Kashi*, Delhi, 1979.

Chapter 6

Conclusion

In India, till today there is not even a single ecomuseum in spite of having great potential for it. To achieve this goal several relevant issues were brought in from chapter 1 to chapter 5. In the Chapter 2, the concept of ecomuseum both in India and abroad and its perspectives in India has been discussed.

The chapter 5 explores Doul Govinda as a sacred complex an exclusive area covering north Guwahati on the north bank of the river Brahmaputra is a significant territory both culturally and ecologically which reveals a distinct local identity. The territory is noted for its vaishnava characteristics resulting in tangible and intangible heritages, historical, archaeological, cultural, linguistic as well as typical north east river ecology. There lie all the ingredients of an ecomuseum in this designated territory.

The intimate association of local communities in preserving their heritage both ecological and cultural and also providing local people with an opportunity to disseminate the significant aspects of habitat and the life style in the Doul Govinda social, cultural and religious contour superimposition of the eco museum concept is addressed here. The potentiality of the Doul Govinda sacred complex, its landscape, both human and natural have been described. The Doul Govinda sacred complex which is pivotal for the preservation of the Assamese culture in its totality appears to be a potential territory revealing exclusive Assamese identity of north Guwahati within a multi cultural city of Guwahati. The typical cultural indicators have been established in respect of the human heritage as the instant marker of local identity in which the sacred complex stands as an interactive centre for the local people as well as outsiders.

The Doul Govinda as a centre of pilgrimage and also has been examined as an integrated institution of Assamese ethnic heritage. There are Anthropological studies on sacred complexes which reveals the advantages of a particular territory to become an eco museum because of the distinctive tangible and intangible heritages connected with the sacred complex as well as voluntary association of the people with the complex. The interrelationship and interconnections of sacred and profane activities within the complex has also been brought into focus. Attempt have been made to understand the relationship between the sacred complex and the villages at large. In what way the common people contributes their mite by way of multiple activities as devotees, as resource person as well as in any other role, having guided by voluntary action in this inter-cultural relationship with the Doul Govinda temple. It has been also experimented how in Indian context sacred complexes have been recognized as the prime institution in giving identity to a territory.

Cultural mapping of the proposed territory has been undertaken. It is a process that facilitates identification of a given territory and their significant heritages. Cultural mapping serves as ethnological atlas. Through cultural mapping of the given territory, systematic documentation is possible in respect of culture and traditions of the territory. It has become helpful in identifying the cultural assets which could be related to the identity of the people of this territory. In other words, by cultural mapping attempt has been made to recognize the significant heritage of the Doul Govinda sacred complex. These heritages are the focal point of an eco museum which reveal the potentiality of the territory as significant parameter for an eco museum.

The territory of Doul Govinda sacred complex has been explored keeping in view the parameters of an ecomuseum postulated by western museologists. In other words, the contour of the given site has been delimited here. It is expected that a given territory must fulfill certain criterion to take the shape of an ecomuseum. Without these criterion or parameters a territory can not be sanctified as an ecomuseum. Thus the site of Doul Govinda sacred complex of north Guwahati, Assam has been subjected to study to find out how these parameters fits into this sacred complex.

The chapter also deals into the structure of Doul Govinda ecomuseum which could be a strategy for the preservation of local identity. Attempt has been made to explore the application of the multi faceted ecomuseum strategy as an alternative mechanism for preserving the cultural elements which are in jeopardy due to changing situation.

The above discussion unveils Doul Govinda sacred complex as a vital and prospective territory for transforming it into an ecomuseum. An attempt has been made in this study to find out the paradigms advocated by ecomuseologists.

Beyond the core area, i.e. the Doul Govinda sacred complex, the religious, social and cultural boundary extends to the city of Guwahati and adjacent villages considering both tangible and intangible heritages emanated the core area. The fragmented nature of ecomuseum gets reflected in this territory. Multiple heritage centres of this territory and their interconnections and integration with the 'head quarter' Doul Govinda sacred complex contributes to the real strength of the territory. The territory is inhabited by a homogenous group of people preserving the typical and hardcore Assamese culture intact, this small cultural pocket has the religious, archaeological, historical, social significance and distinctiveness. Ecologically the territory is unique due to the interface of a river ecology and a hilly undulating terrain gradually merging with the eastern Himalayan ranges in the north. The territory endure the archaeological evidences of even 9th-10th cent. AD. Historical significance of the territory lies in the fact that it remained administrative head quarter for the rulers of Assam. Metaphorically the territory is known as the 'Kashi of the East'. It is considered as religious hub and occupies the centre stage in the lives of people. This is an area in the vicinity of the powerful 'sakti pitha'-kamakhya completely influenced by vaishnava tradition. This significant religious faith can be felt virtually in every aspect of social life of the people. The religious centres of the territory are the centers of sacred and profane activities. The interconnections of these activities contribute to the local identity strengthen by these institutions.

The weaknesses include lack of awareness among the people of the territory as well as the concept of ecomuseum. They are not aware how gradually they are loosing their local identity. As has been mentioned earlier that the territory which is a small pocket where rich cultural heritage of Assam has remained untouched in spite of being part of the multicultural Guwahati city. But people are still unaware and less concern of their heritage. The territory known as 'kashi of the east' in Assam receives highest attention for its significant religious contribution. However, people here do not show their concern over their privileges. Few tourist ventures into this area that to occasionally for *darshan*. There is no infrastructure for the tourist as such.

There are tremendous opportunities lying in this territory for heritage conservation and dissemination. In fact, the whole territory itself is a museum without wall. It requires only systematic approach and effort. The territory accommodates several sacred centres which come under the purview of Doul Govinda sacred complex. These centres refer to the concept of fragmented museum. Besides there are ecological advantages also. The Brahmaputra river has converted the territory into an isolated pocket. Thus, the tangible and intangible heritage of the people still remain untouched. All the archaeological, historical evidence are the ready reference for a significant territory and great opportunity for an ecomuseum. The sacred centres, specially the Doul Govinda temple receives hundreds of local devotees everyday. Hence, the local people have tremendous opportunities to reap the benefit of their skills in the form of performing art, craft practices and so on. Besides, people can build up their own heritage club or sacred corners where they can preserve their inimitable heritage. The whole idea will ultimately help in the preservation of the 'local identity' in terms of heritages both man made and nature made.

The threats lying underneath are equally of major concern. Many development activities taking place in this territory in a rapid pace in recent time. The Indian Institute of Technology (IIT), North East chapter has been established in this area, which is bringing changes not only in the socio-economic sphere of life but also in the behavioural pattern and culture also. Due to developed communication, the isolation of this pocket is gradually braking up. Thus the barricade between north and south Guwahati is disappearing. It has incorporated many outside elements to this typical Assamese culture surviving onslaught of time. Besides, the socio cultural conflict and activities of certain radical groups could be another major threat for this territory because it acts as diluents to the outside tourist to venture into this territory.

It has been observed from the above analysis that the concept of the ecomuseum in Doul Govinda sacred complex in terms of significant territory , local identity, heritage conservation, people's participation, head quarter antennae interface and the regeneration of the collective memory could be an appropriate strategy for conserving local traditions, ecology etc. as well as for dissemination. Besides, potentiality is tremendous, all the integrated elements within the contour of an ecomuseum which is apparent gives the present analysis could be considered as the right opportunity. Thus, with the systematic and professional approach the territory of Doul Govinda sacred complex can be a unique ecomuseum in India.

Appendix-I

Distribution of population.

Sl no.	District	Ward	Village	Castes
1.	Kamrup	3	Shilsako	General OBC
2.	-do-	3	Madhyamkhanda	General OBC
3.	-do-	4	Rajaduar	SC OBC General

Appendix-II

Religious calendar

Sl. No.	Name of the religious festival	Month of occurrence	The function days	Celebrated at the level	Deities worshipped	Performer
1.	Magh bihu	January	2 days	Village, household	Agni	Village members
2.	Saraswati puja	February	1 day	Schools	Goddess Saraswati	Priest and students
3.	Shivratri	March	1 day	Village	Shiva	Priest, household members
4.	Holi	March	5 days	Household and village	Krishna	Villagers
5.	Bahag bihu	April	7 days	Household and village	Household deity	Household members
6.	SankarDev & MadhavDev	September	1 day	Namghar	Sankar Dev and Madhav Dev	Villagers
7.	Janmastami	September	1 day	Household and namghar	Krishna	Villagers and household members
8.	Durga puja	Oct-Nov	4 days	Village	Goddess Durga	Village members
9.	Lakshmi puja	Oct- Nov	1 day	Household and village	Goddess Lakshmi	Household members
10.	Kali puja	Oct-Nov	1 day	Village	Goddess Kali	Villagers
11.	Diwali	Oct-Nov	1 day	Household	Household deity	Household members

Glossary

Ankiya nat	one act play
Arati	singing devotional songs
Arcana	to worship
Avatara	incarnation
Bandana	to praise
Bargit	type of devotional songs composed by Sankaradeva
Bhakta	devotees
Bhawana	dance drama performed in *namgharas*
Bhog	eatables offered to deity
Birina	a type of grass bush
Buranji	history
Chaki	lamp
Deva	the god
Faku	coloured powder
Ghosha	devotional songs
Guru	the teacher
Hari bhakti	devotion to god
Haveli	palace
Jnyana	wisdom
Karma	deeds
Kirttana	to recite

Monikut	sanctum sanctorium
Nama	religious songs
Namghar	vaishnava temple
Oza-pali	a type of sacred performances
Prasad	transcendent food
Puja	worship
Pukhuri	Lake
Raksas	demon
Sakhitwa	to friendship
Satradhikar	head of satra
Sayan	to rest
Smarana	to remember
Srawana	to listen
Tamol	Betel nut (Areca catasu)
Tantrik	magician
Tulsi	basil leaf
Upacaras	offerings

Bibliography

Agarwal, V.S., *Harshacharitra – Ek Sanskritic Adhyayan*, Bihar Rashtra Bhasa Parisad, Patna, 1964

Anon, 'The Ecomuseum', *Newsletter of the ICOM Natural History Committee*, 1978

'*Aspects of the Heritage of Assam : A Souvenir*', (edited volume), Indian History Congress, Guwahati, 1959

Banerjee, N. R., *Museum and Cultural Heritage in India*, Agam Kala Prakashan. Delhi, 1990

Barua, B.K., *A Cultural History of Assam (early period)*, Vol I, Bina Library, Guwahati, 2003

Barua, Krishnamurti, *Karmajogi Prafulla Ch. Barooah*, Tribune Press, Guwahati, 1992

Barua, P.C., 'North Guwahati where Time has Stood Still', *The Assam Tribune*, Tribune Press, Guwahati, 1985

Basham, A.L. (ed.) *A Cultural History of India*, Clarendon Press, Oxford. 1975

Bedekar, V.H., *New Museology for India*, National Museum Institute, New Delhi, 1995

Bhatnagar, A., *Museum, Museology and New Museology*, S.B. Enterprise, New Delhi, 1999

Boylan, Ptrick J.(ed.), *Museums 2000: Politics, People, Professionals and Profit*, Museums Association, Routledge, London and New York, 1992

----------------------- 'Ecomuseums and the new museology – some definitions', *Museum Journal* 92(4), 1992

Breckenridge, C. A. and Appadurai, A., 'Museums are Good to Think. Heritage on View in India', in Boswell,D., and Evans Jessica (ed.) *Representing the Nation: A Reader*, Routledge, London and New York, 1999

Carbonell, B.M. (ed.), *Museum Studies, An Anthology of Contexts*, Blackwell Publishing Ltd. United Kingdom, 2004

Choudhury, P.C., *The History of Civilization of the People of Assam to the Twelve Century AD*, Department of Historical and Antiquarian Studies in Assam, Gauhati, 1966

Choudhury, R.D., *Art Heritage of Assam*, Aryan Books International, New Delhi 1998.

----------------------- *Sculptural Heritage of Assam*, National Museum, Janpath, New Delhi, 2000

Corsane, G. (ed.), *Heritage, Museums and Galleries, Introductory Reader*, Routledge, New york, 2005.

Corsane, G. and Holleman, W. 'Ecomuseums: a brief evaluation', In R. De Jong, (ed.) *Museums and the Environment*, South African Museums Association, Pretoria, 1993

Das, B.M., *The Peoples of Assam*, Gian Publishing House, 29/6 Shakti Nagar, Delhi, 1968

Dutt, K.N. (ed.), *Aspects of the Heritage of Assam*, Indian History Congress, Guwahati, Dec' 1959

Davis, P., *Ecomuseums A Sense of Place*, Leicester University Press, London and New York, 1999

Dwivedi, V. P. and Pant G.N.,(ed.), *Museums and Museology: New Horizon*, Agam Kala Prakashan, Delhi, 1980

Edson, Gary (ed.), *Museum Ethics*, Routledge, London and New York, 1997

Edson, Gary and David Dean, *The Handbook for Museums*, Routledge, London and New York, 1994

Fladmark, J.M. (ed.), *Heritage and Museums Shaping National Identity*, Heritage Library, The Robert Gordon University, 1999.

Gait, Edward, *A History of Assam,* Bina Library, Guwahati, 1926

Ghosh, S.K.(ed), *Ramayana in the North-east India*, B.R. Publishing Corporation, Delhi, 2002

Greenhill, E. H. (ed.), *Cultural Diversity. Developing Museum Audiences in Britain*, Leicester University Press, London and Washington, 1997

Harris, Marvin, *The Rise of Anthropological Theory*, Routledge and Kegan Paul, London, 1968

Hooper-Greenhill, E., *Museums and the Interpretation of Visual Culture*, Routledge, London and New York, 2000

Kaplan, Flora, E. S. (ed.), *Museums and the Making of ''ourselves''*. Leicester University Press, London and New York, 1996

Lal, Chaman, *India – Cradle of Cultures*, Modern school, New Delhi, 1966

'*Mahaprabhu Shri Shri Doul Govinda Mandir'r Ititbritta aru Aitihasik Uttar Guwahati'r Smritisihna*' - a bilingual information broucher published by Doul Govinda Temple Trust, Guwahati, 2002

Nath, Rajmohan, *The Background of Assamese Culture*, Dutta Baruah & Co, Gauhati, 1978

Neog, Maheswar, *Sankaradeva*, National Book Trust, Delhi, 1967

Poddar, H.P., (ed.) *Mahabharat*, Geeta Press, Gorakhpur, 1955

Riviere, G. H., 'the Ecomuseum: an evolutive definition', *Museum*, 37(4), 1985

Rivard, R. 'Museuma and ecomuseums-questions and answers', in J.A.Gjestrum and M. Maure (ed.) *Ukomuseumsboka – identiest, okologi, deltakelse*, ICOM, Tromso, Norway, 1988

Sarma, S.N., *The Neo-Vaisnavite Movement and the Satra Institution of Assam*, Lawyer's Book Stall, Panbazar, Guwahati

Shamasastry, R., (Trnsl), *Kautilya's Arthasastra*, Mysore Printing and Publishing House, Mysore, 1967

Shastri, B.,(ed.) *Kalikapurane Murtivinirdesah*, IGNCA, Delhi, 1994

Susan M. Pearce, (ed.) *Museum Studies in Material Culture*, Leicester University Press, London, 19

Van Mensch, P.J.A., 'Museology and the Management of the Natural and Cultural Heritage'. In R. De Jong, (ed.) *Museums and the Environment*, South African Museums Association, Pretoria, 1993.

Varine, H.de, *Ecomuseums or community museums? 25 years of applied research in Museology and Development*, Nordisk Museologi, 1996.

Vidyarthi, L.P., *The Sacred Complex of Hindu Gaya*, Asia Publishing House, Bombay, 1961

_____________ *The Maler - A Study In Nature Man Spirit Complex of A Hill Tribe in Bihar*, Bookland Private Limited, Calcutta: Patna : Allahabad

Vidyarthi, L.P. et.el, *The Sacred Complex of Kashi*, Concept Publishing Company, Delhi, 1979

Viet, J. (ed.) *The International Thesaurus of Cultural Development*, Clearing House and Research Center for Cultural Development, UNESCO, Paris, 1980

www.Tribuneindia.com/2001/spectrum/main/2htm.February 2009

www.norway.cn/environment/developement+cooperation/ecomuseum.htm

www.skyecomuseum.co.uk/childrens-ecomuseum.php

www.town.sobetsu.hokkaido.jp/eco/ecomirai

www.ekomuseum.se/english/besokmal

www.ekomuseum.dk/english

www.halong.gov.vn/details: asp

http:/213.254.4.222/cataloghi/pd fires/535:

www.staffin.net/pdfs/staffin

www.osservatorioecomusei.net/start.php

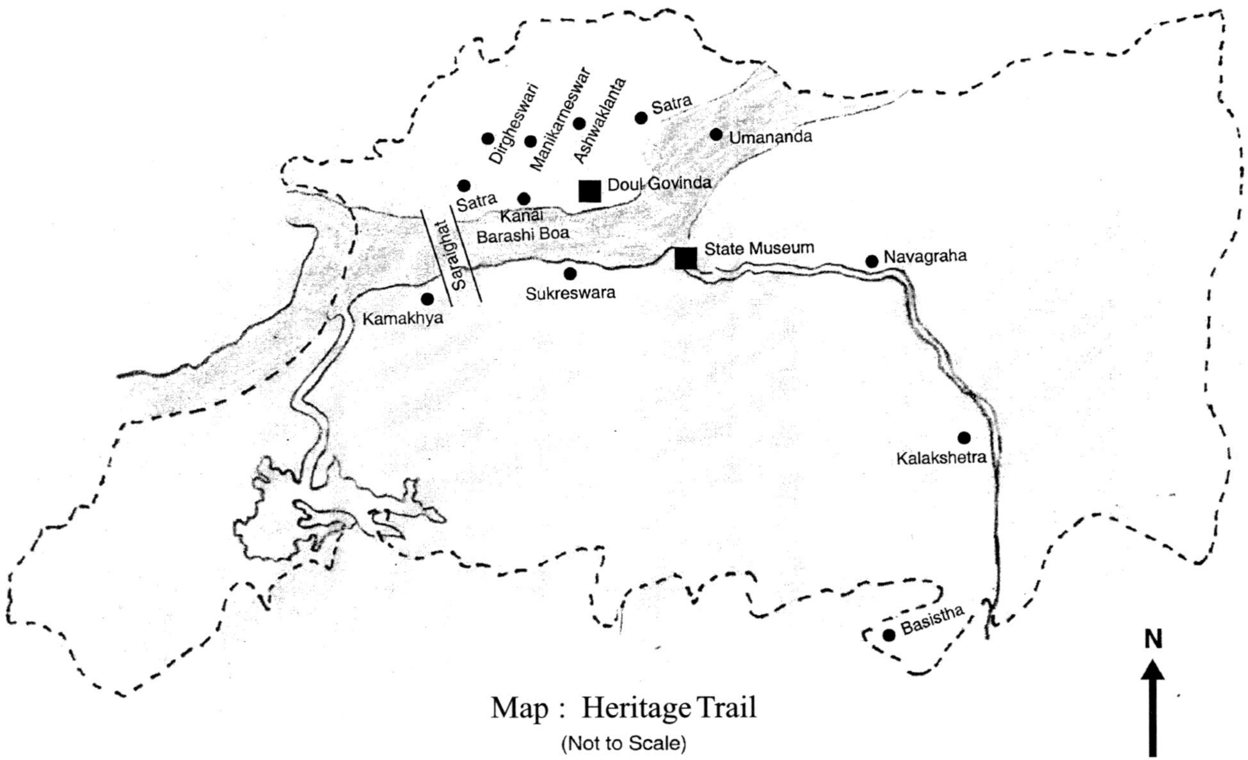

Map : Heritage Trail
(Not to Scale)

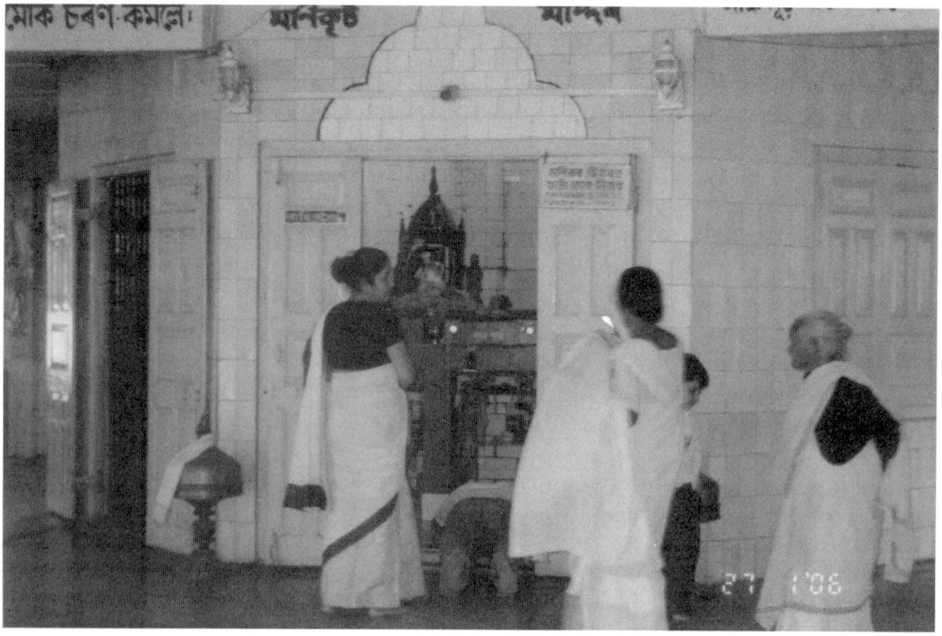

Pl. 1 : The sanctum sanctorum

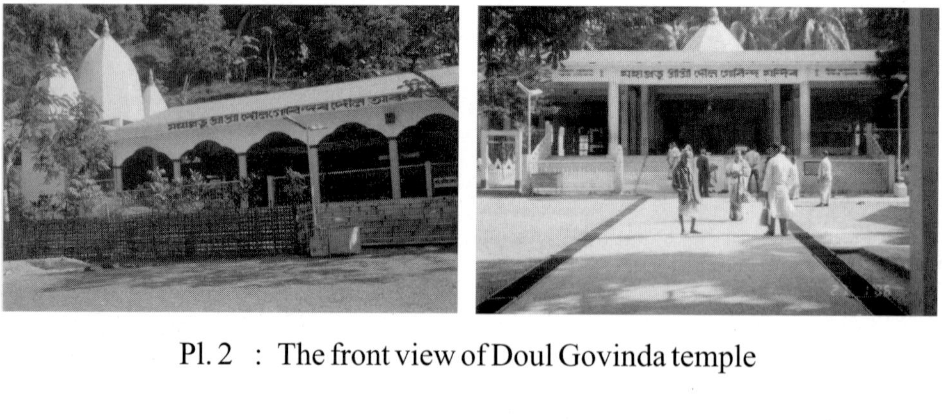

Pl. 2 : The front view of Doul Govinda temple

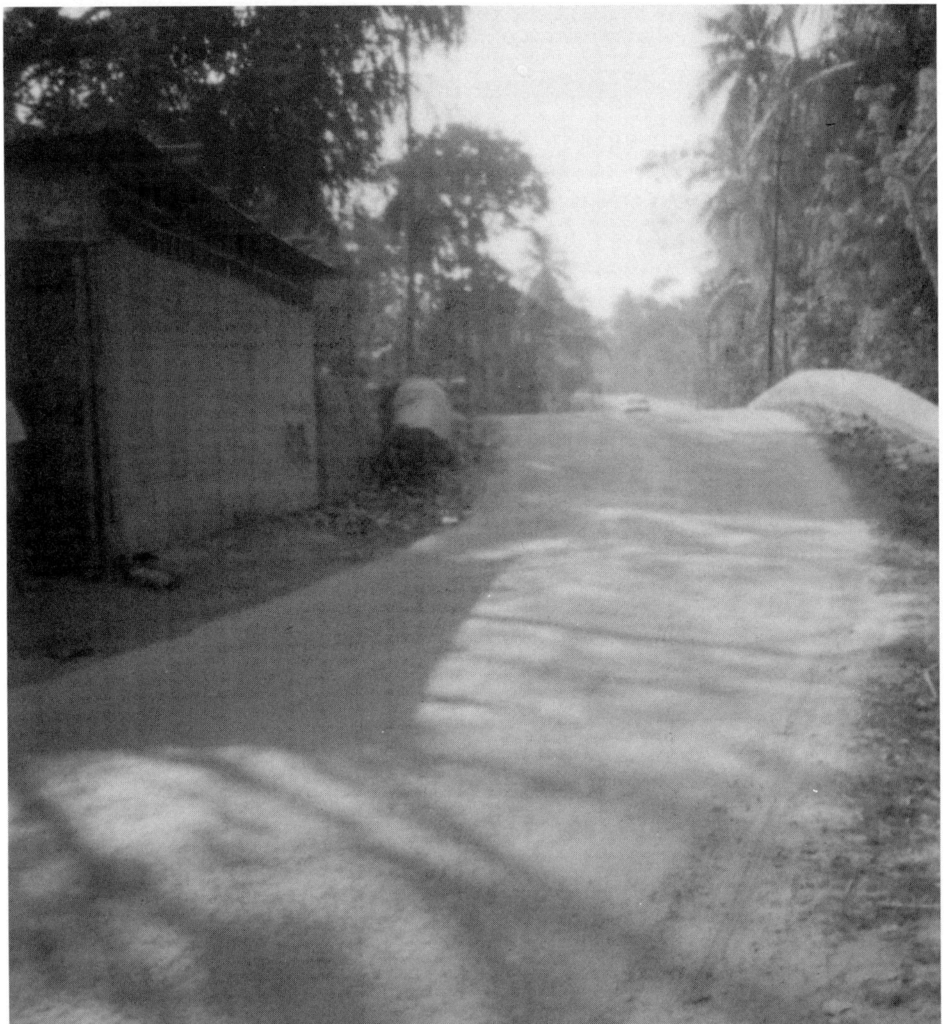

Pl. 3 : Remains of Shilsako

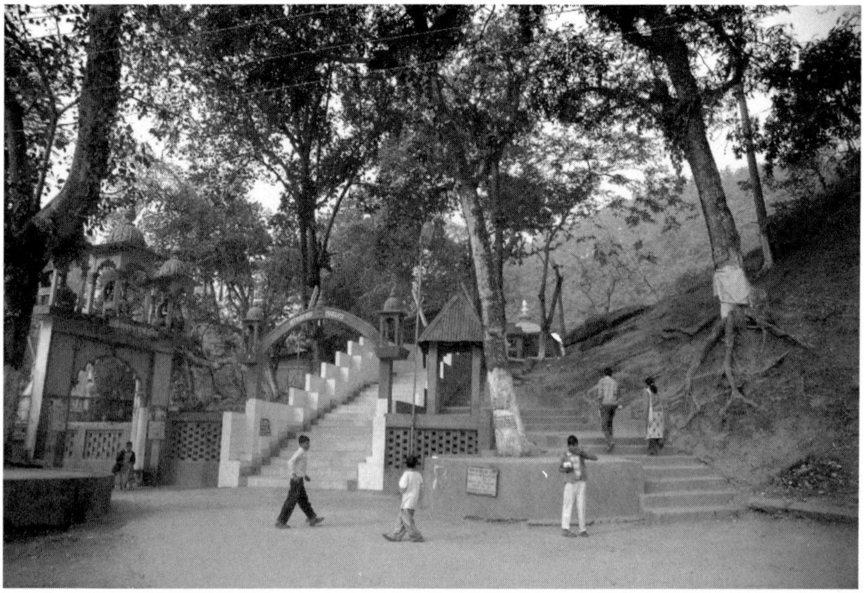

Pl. 4 : Vasisthashram

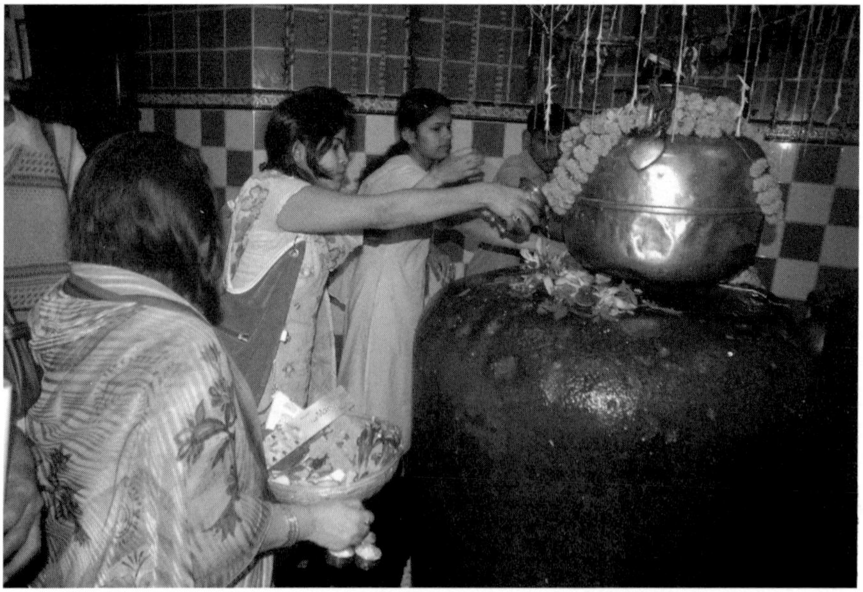

Pl. 5 : Devotees praying the Shivlinga of Sukreswar

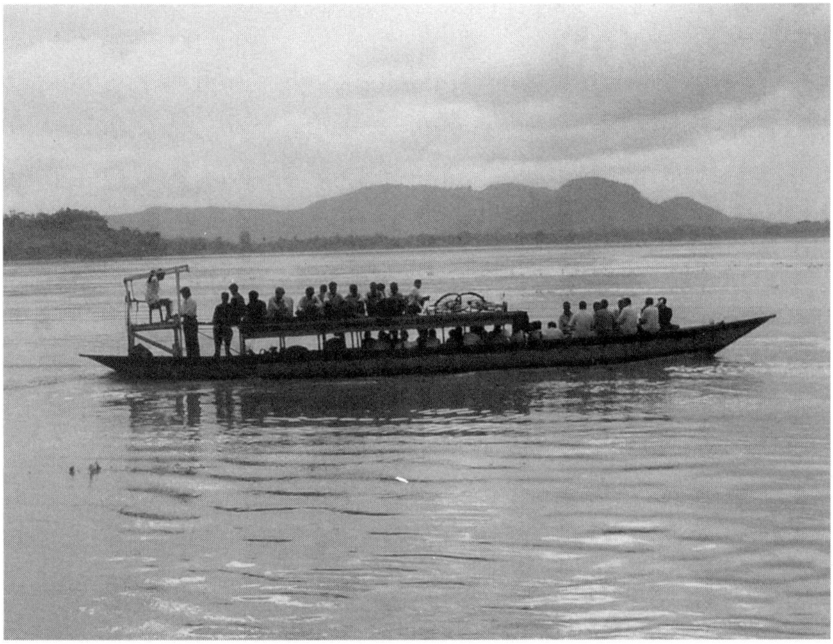

Pl. 6 : Crossing Brahmaputra in a steamer

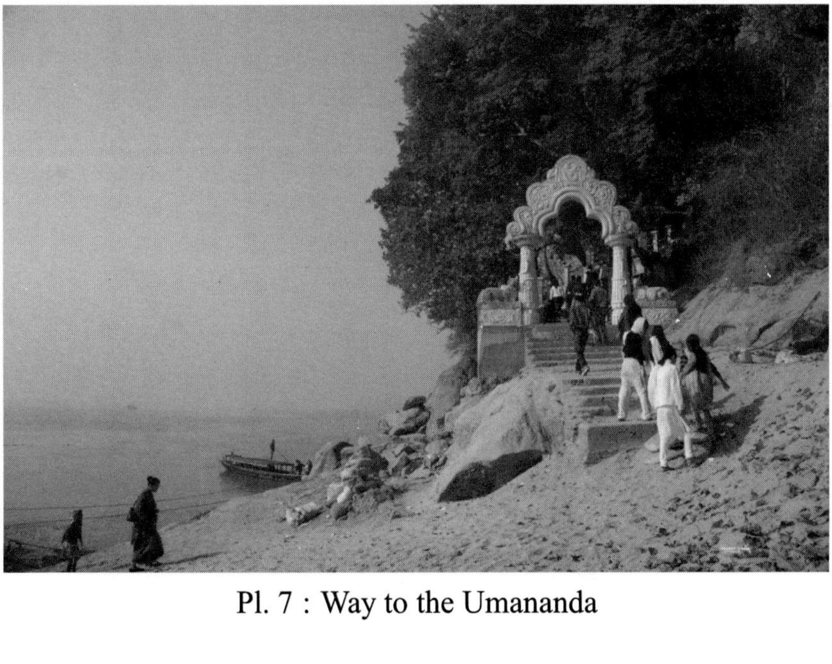

Pl. 7 : Way to the Umananda

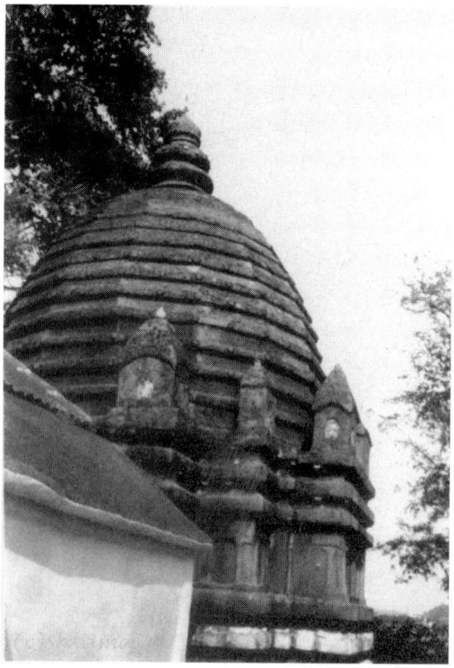

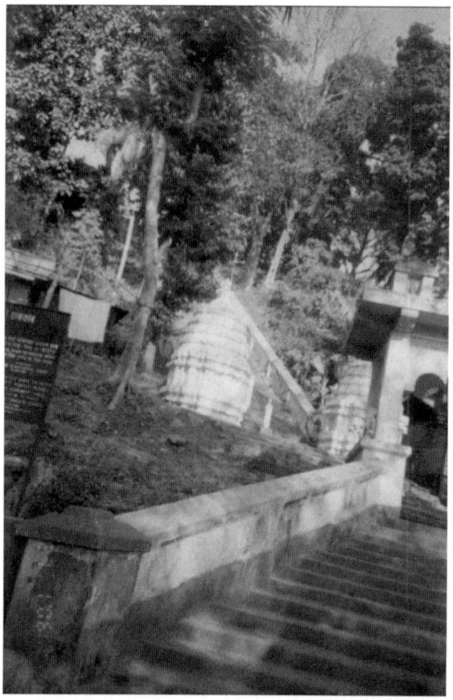

Pl. 8 : The Ashwaklanta

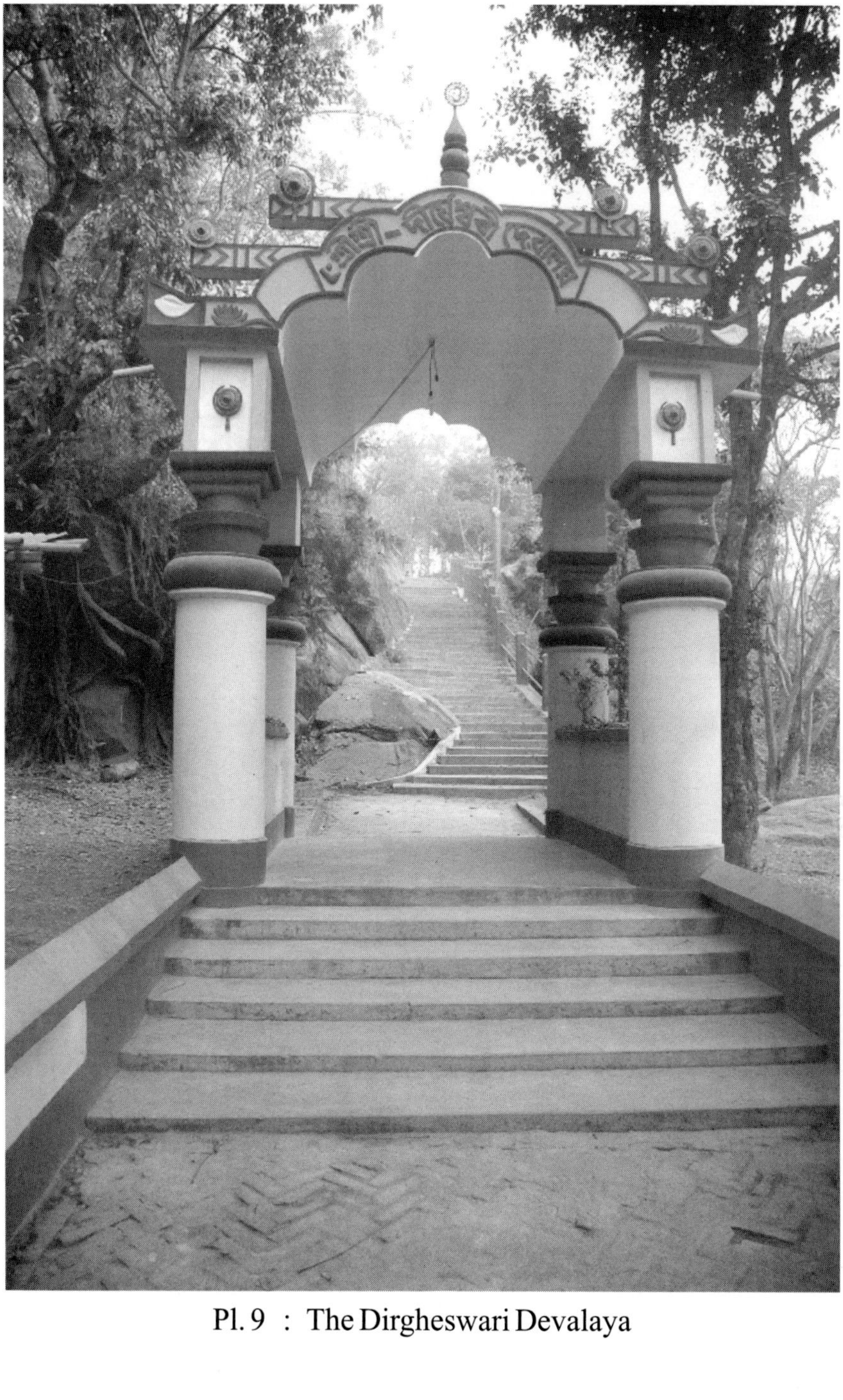

Pl. 9 : The Dirgheswari Devalaya

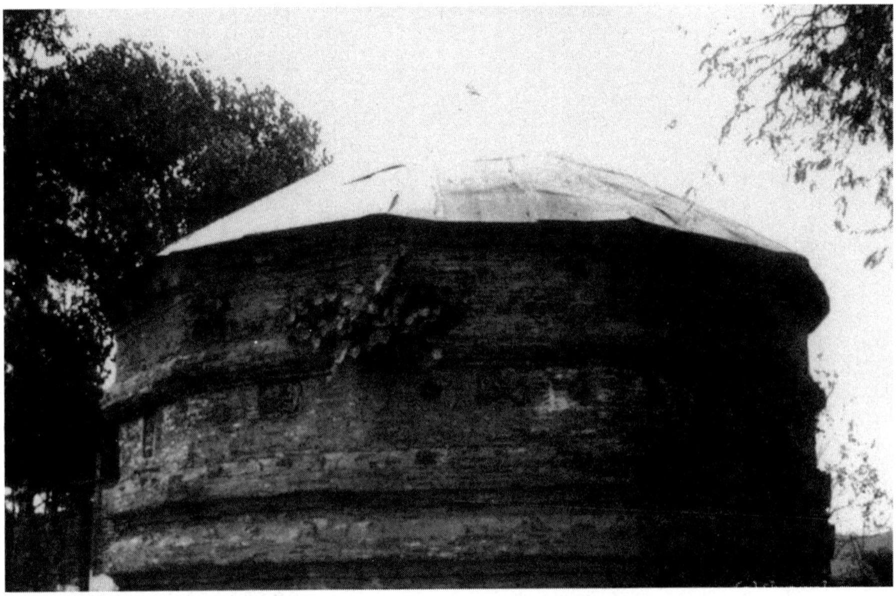

Pl. 10 : The Manikarneswar

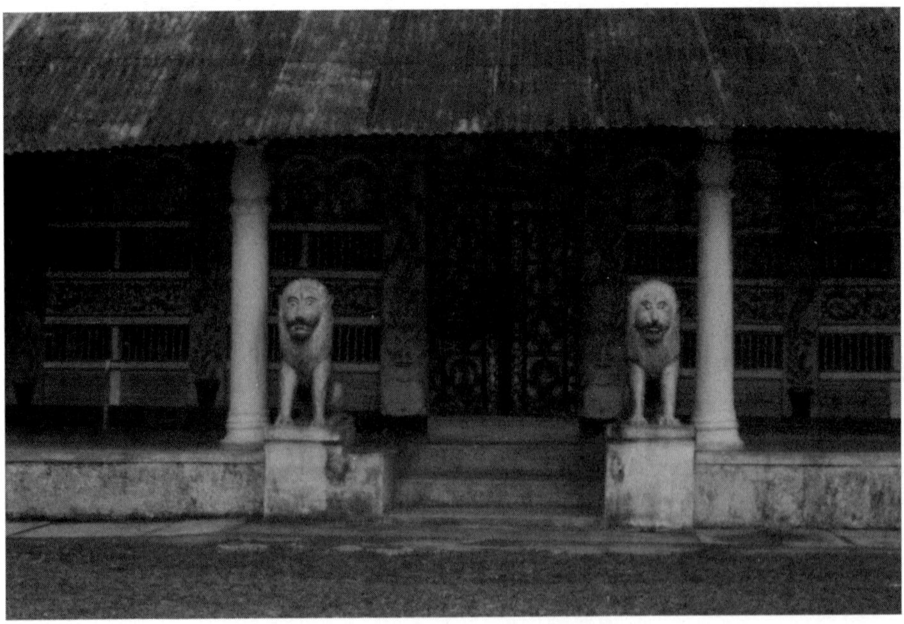

Pl. 11 : Entrance of a Satra

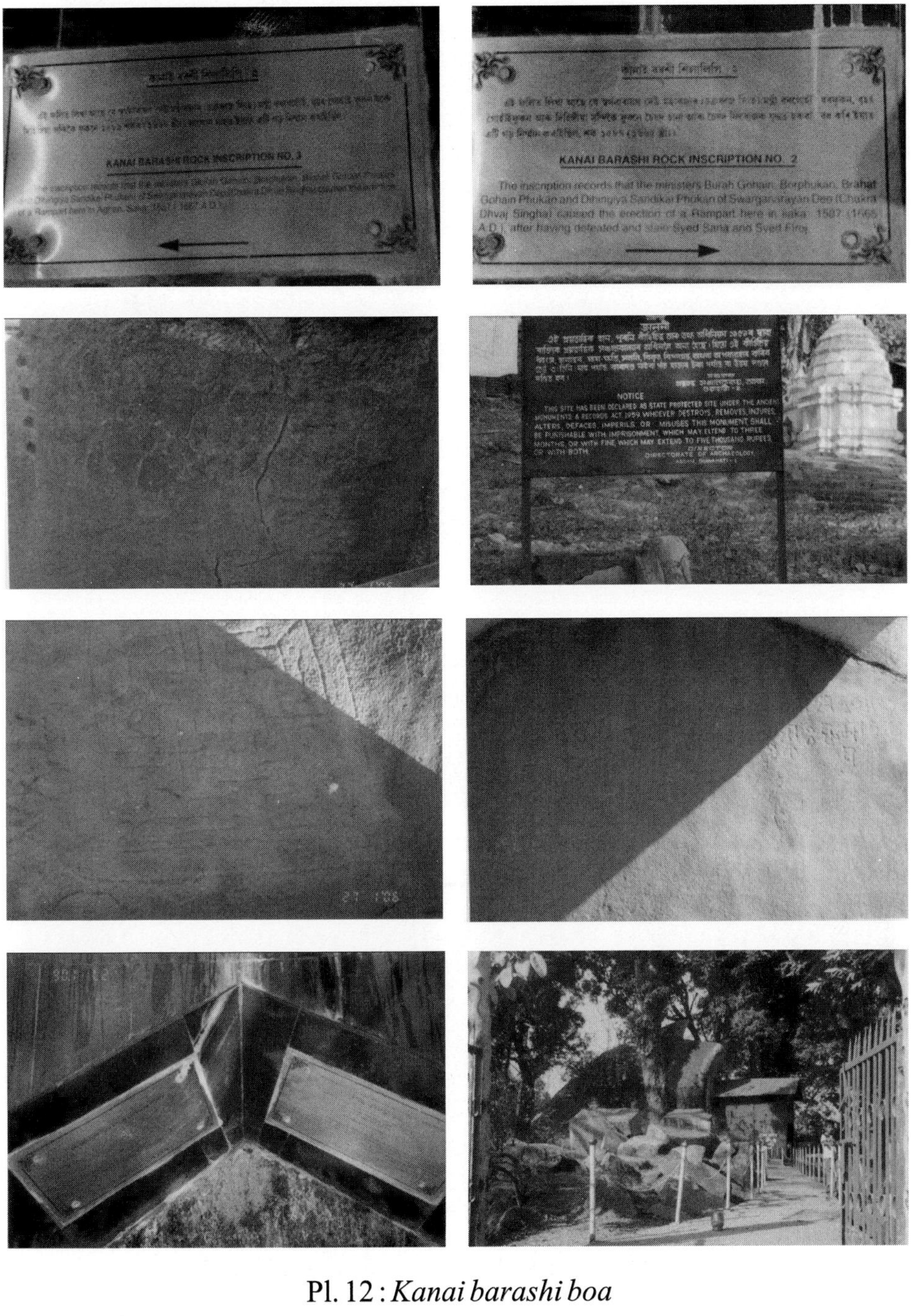

Pl. 12 : *Kanai barashi boa*

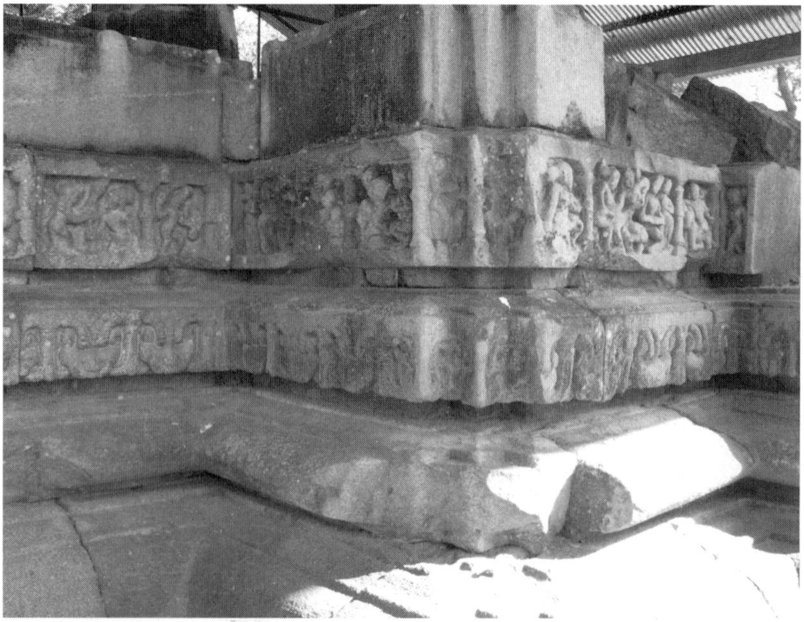

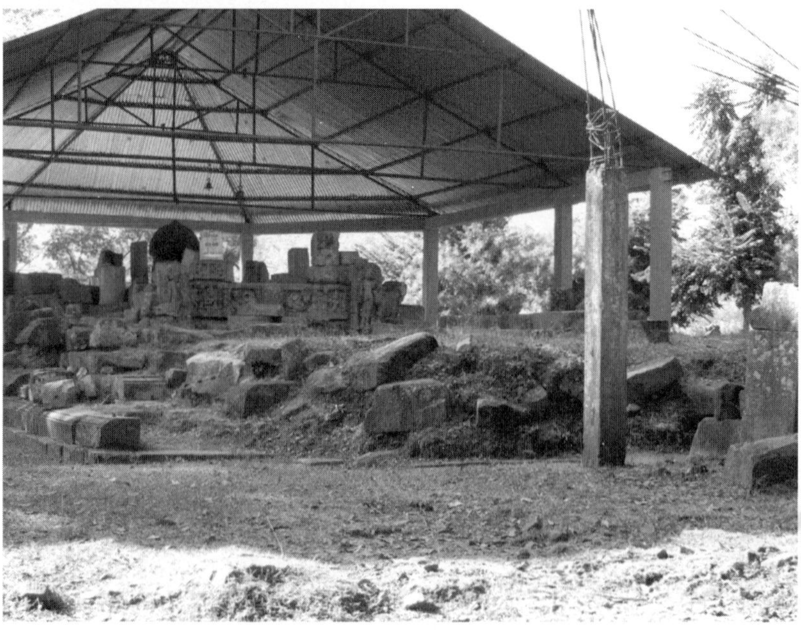

Pl. 13 : Archaeological remains of Madan Kamdev

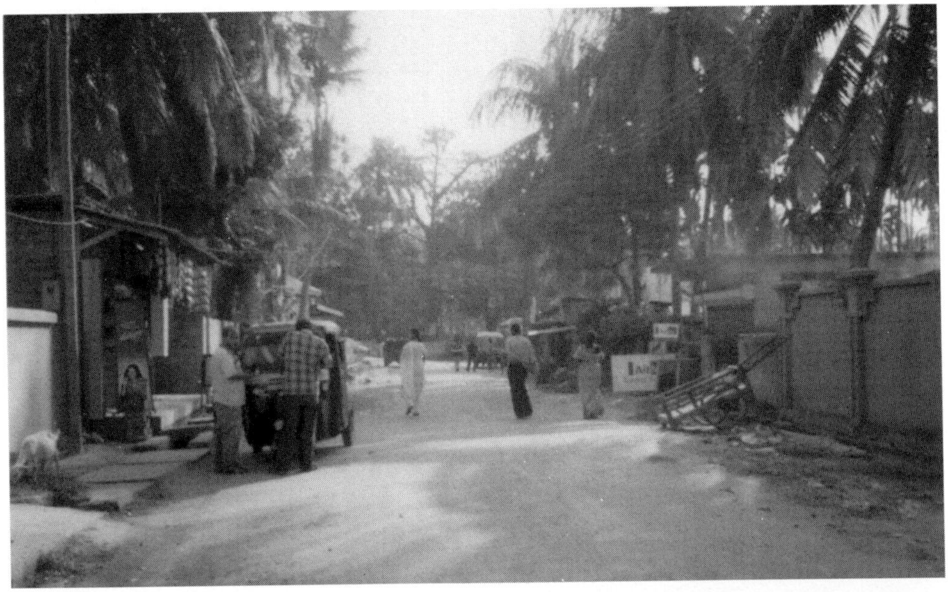

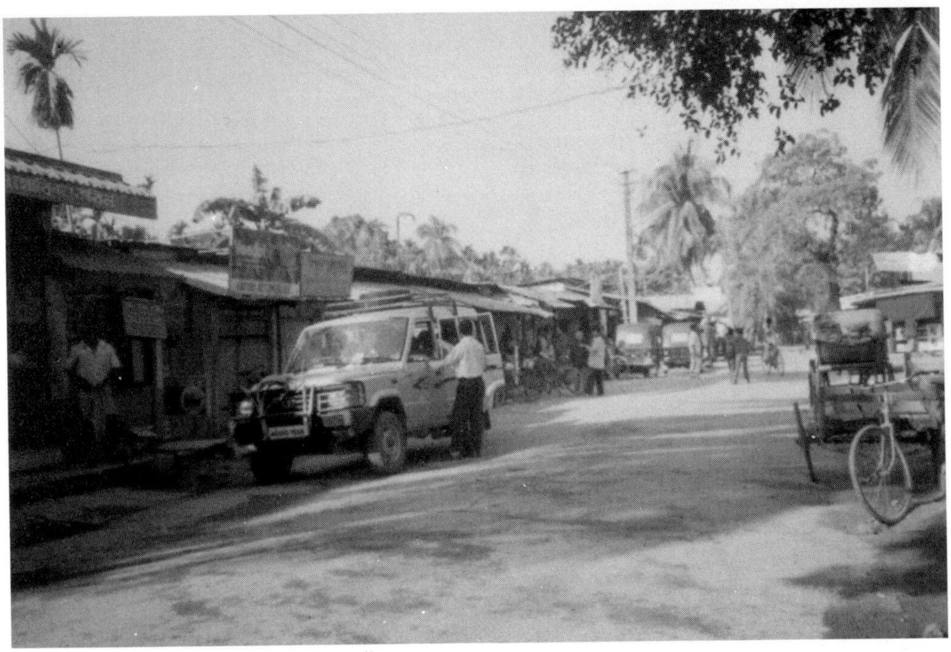

Pl. 14 : Urbanisation

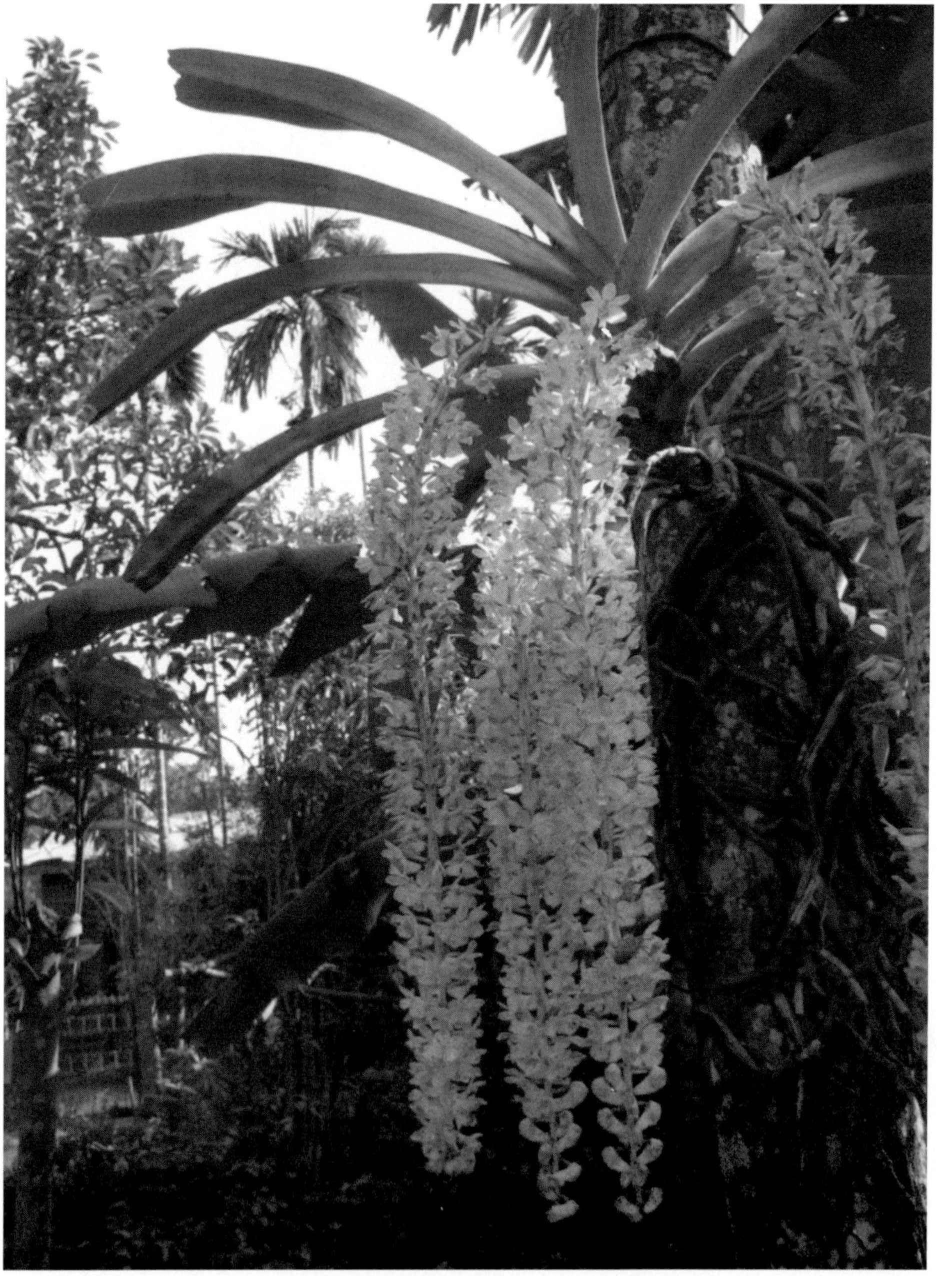

Pl. 15 : Kapou Phul: An Orchid

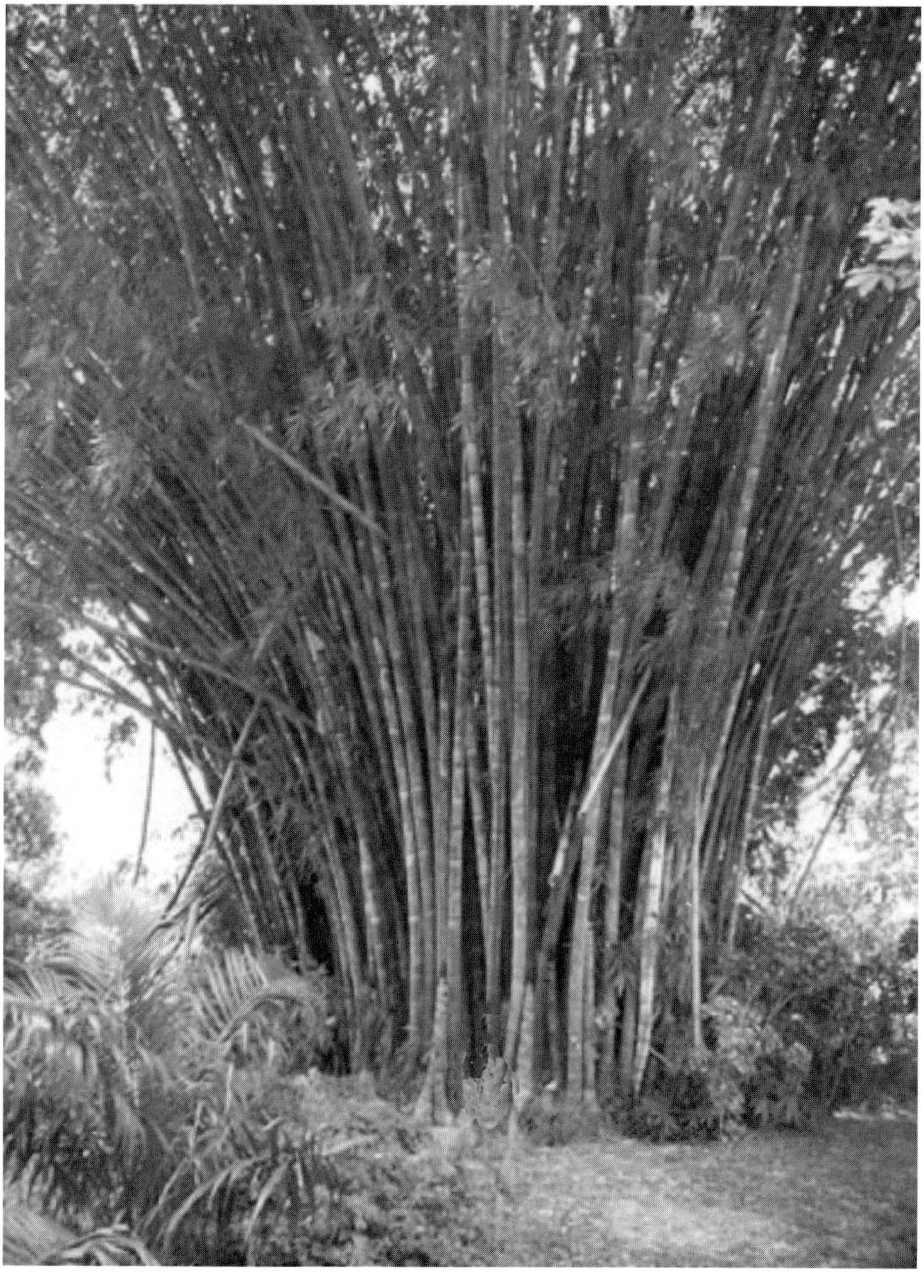

Pl. 16 : A Bamboo Tree

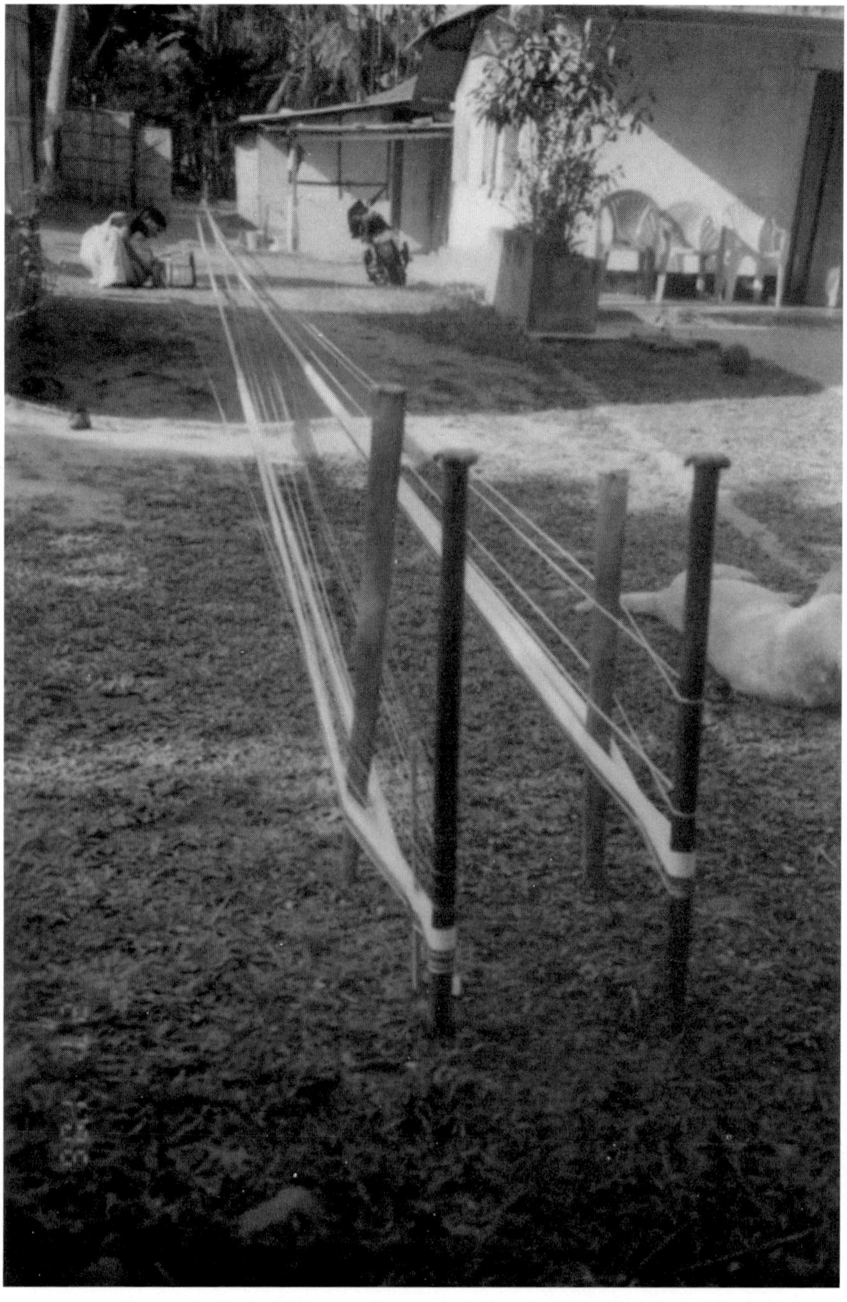

Pl. 17 : Preparation for weaving Gamocha in a handloom

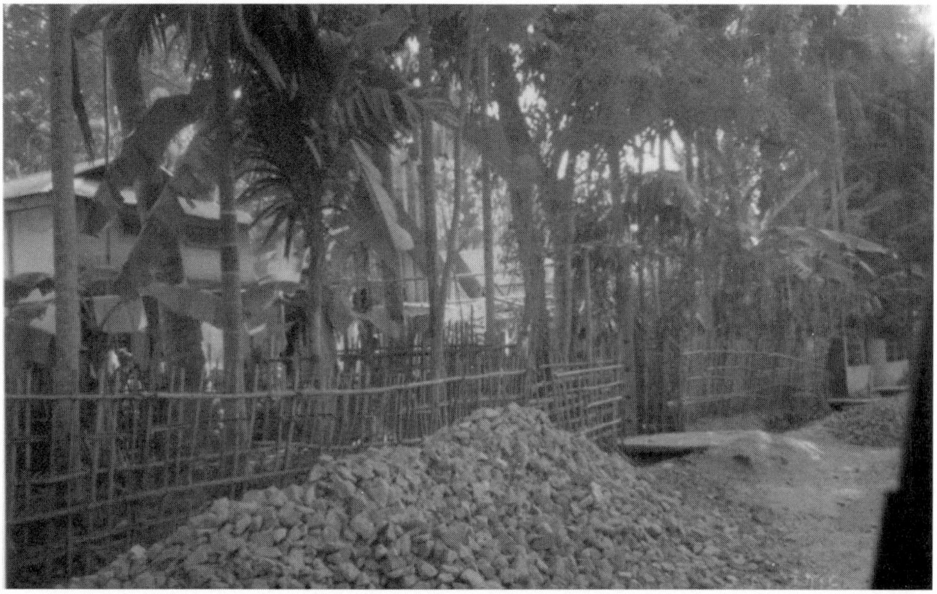

Pl. 18 : The Village Life

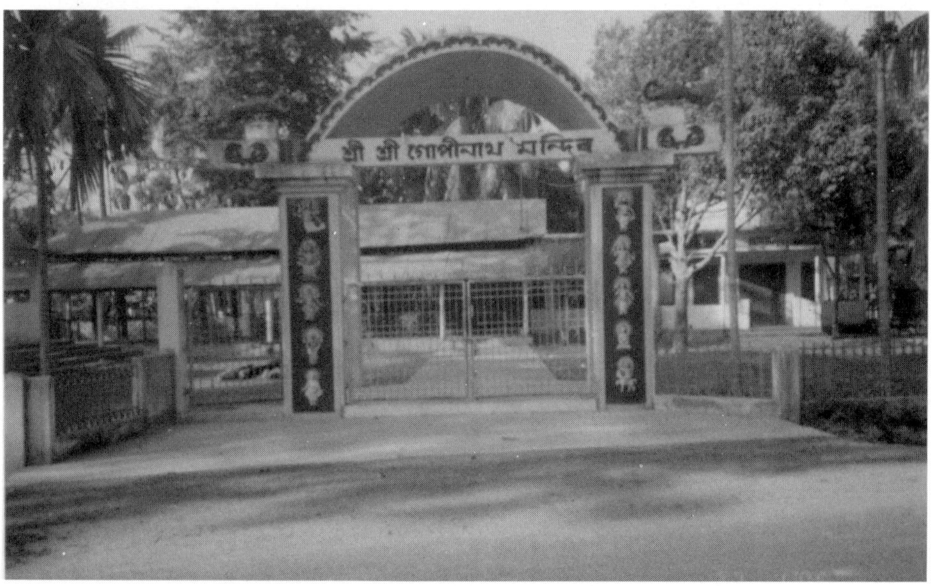

Pl. 19 : Other Religious Centers in North Guwahati

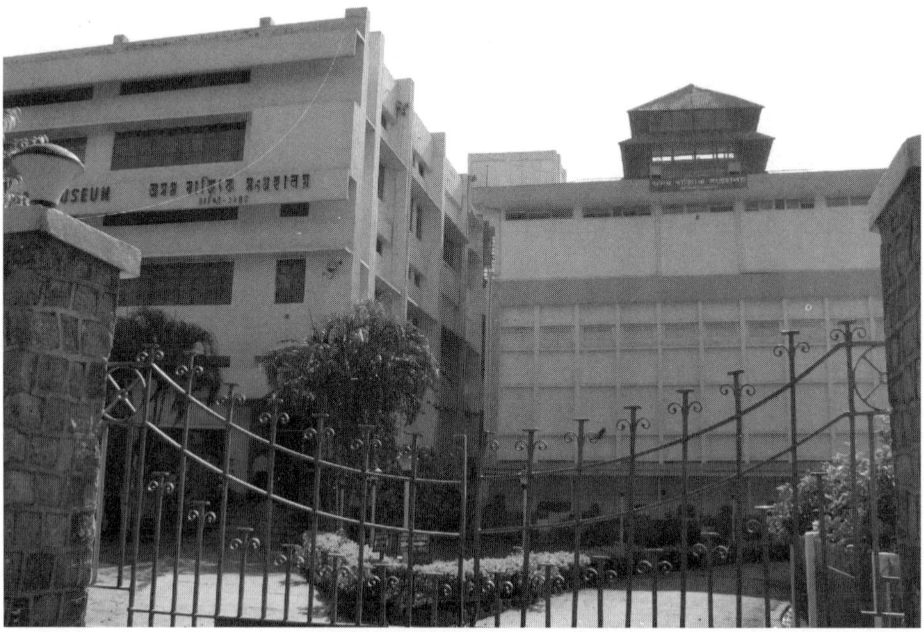

Pl. 20 : Front view of Assam State Museum